GENESIS

PART I: GOD AND HIS CREATION
GENESIS 1-11

by Gayle Somers with Sarah Christmyer

EMMAUS ROAD PUBLISHING

Steubenville, Ohio
A Division of Catholics United for the Faith

Emmaus Road Publishing
827 North Fourth Street
Steubenville, Ohio 43952

Library of Congress Control Number: 2004113091
ISBN 1-931018-22-7

Cover design and layout by
Beth Hart

Cover artwork:
Michelangelo, *The Creation of Adam* (detail)

To the Women's Bible Study of
St. Thomas the Apostle Catholic Church
in Phoenix, Arizona—the most beautiful guinea pigs
on the face of the planet

—Gayle Somers

To my grandparents,
David and Helen Morken,
who walked with God

—Sarah Christmyer

Table of Contents

Preface

Hearts Aflame Scripture Study

I n the last chapter of Luke's Gospel, we have a wonderful account of a Catholic Bible study. It was the day of the Resurrection, and Luke tells us that two of Jesus' disciples were heading out from Jerusalem to a nearby town called Emmaus. They were "talking with each other" about all the things that had just happened. Mysteriously, "Jesus himself drew near and went with them. But their eyes were kept from recognizing him" (Lk. 24:15–16). He asked them what they were discussing. With a mixture of sadness and confusion, they told Him how their high hopes for Jesus had been dashed with the Crucifixion. They also told Him there was a report by some of the women that the tomb in which He had been buried was empty when they visited it; they hardly knew what to make of that.

Jesus chided them for their foolishness and their denseness: "O foolish men, and slow of heart to believe all that the prophets have spoken!" (Lk. 24:25). The remedy for their malaise was right under their noses, so to speak—in the Scriptures. Starting with the first book of the Old Testament, Jesus interpreted it all for them, showing how all its words, which surely were so familiar to them as Jews, had a much deeper meaning than they realized. He showed them how all of it was about Him, making it clear that everything that had happened to Him, including the Crucifixion, had been foretold.

When the company reached their destination, the two disciples, still unaware of Jesus' identity, begged Him not to go any farther. "Stay with us," they urged Him (Lk. 24:29). Their "Bible study" had deeply affected them; they didn't want to let this man out of their sight.

And so Jesus went in to stay with them. "When he was at table with them, he took the bread and blessed, and broke it, and gave it to them. And their eyes were opened and they recognized Him" (Lk. 24:30–31). He was gone in a flash, but the disciples' dazzling experience with Him on the road, as they listened to Him teach them from Scripture, lingered with them. "Did not our hearts burn within us while he talked to us on the road, while he opened to us the scriptures?" (Lk. 24:32) Energized by this encounter with the resurrected Jesus, they rushed back to Jerusalem "that same hour" to make a report to the apostles about what had happened to them. The Eleven had already gotten the good news, because the Lord had appeared to Peter, too. The Emmaus disciples "told what had happened on the road, and how he was known to them in the breaking of the bread" (24:35). A Bible study *and* the Eucharist had fully revealed Jesus to them.

From that day to this, the Church has told us that there are two ways of "knowing" Jesus—through Word and Sacrament. We see this, for example, in the Mass. "The Church has always venerated the divine Scriptures just as she venerates the body of the Lord, since, especially in the sacred liturgy, she unceasingly receives and offers to the faithful the bread of life from the table both of God's word and of Christ's body."[1] The witness of the saints confirms this: "I have a question for you, brothers and sisters. Which do you think more important—the word of God or the body of Christ? If you want to answer correctly, you must tell me that the word of God is not less important than the body of Christ! How careful we are, when the body of Christ is distributed to us, not to let any bit of it fall to the ground from our hand! But we should be just as careful not to let slip from our hearts the word of God."[2]

Although Catholic liturgy and tradition preserve a proper reverence for Scripture, the "burning heart" produced by the glorious Bible study on the Emmaus road still eludes many Catholics today. Hearts Aflame Scripture Study aims to help Catholics recover their heritage of lives energized by the illumination, wisdom, and presence of Jesus in His Word. Bible study is a profoundly Catholic thing to do.

Hearts Aflame Scripture Study

Hearts Aflame Scripture Study is built upon the conviction that the Scripture is not a textbook, even though we "study" it; rather, it is a place of encounter with God. "For in the sacred books, the Father who is in heaven meets His children with great love and speaks with them; and the force and power in the word of God is so great that it stands as the support and energy of the Church, the strength of faith for her sons, the food of the soul, the pure and everlasting source of spiritual life."[3] We don't approach the Bible simply to get information. We want to have a genuine experience of entering into the loving conversation that God desires to have with us in His Word. We expect to be as riveted by this as those disciples on the road to Emmaus were. We understand that our recognition of Jesus in the sacraments will be enriched and deepened by encountering Him "on the road," as we read the Scriptures. We are looking beyond information to *transformation*. How will that happen?

Encountering Jesus in the Scripture takes *time*, just as it did for the disciples on the road to Emmaus. Although their hearts were burning as they listened to the Stranger teach them the Scripture, it was only when they extended their visit with Him by invit-

---

[1] Second Vatican Council, Dogmatic Constitution on Divine Revelation *Dei Verbum* (November 18, 1965), no. 21.
[2] Saint Caesarius of Arles, Sermon 300.2.
[3] *Dei Verbum*, no. 21.

ing Him to stay that He fully revealed Himself to them. This is instructive for us. It helps us to see that patience, curiosity, hospitality, and humility are all important when we seek to know Jesus in His Word. Hearts Aflame Scripture Study is a measured approach to Scripture. It is text-centered, requiring numerous readings of the same passage. It includes opportunities to open our hearts to the fire of God's love, communicated through the supernatural text of the Bible. It encourages lingering over the text even after a lesson is completed, inviting Jesus to "stay with us" just a little longer. All the elements of Hearts Aflame Scripture Study are designed to help us imitate the Blessed Virgin Mary, who stored up in her heart everything concerning Jesus that she heard and saw and experienced. She pondered the mighty works of God, and so will we.

How to Use This Study

Here is how the material in each lesson is organized:

At the beginning of each lesson, there is an introduction that gives just enough background information to get you started—but only enough to whet the appetite. The sooner you get to the passage to read the words and think about them, the more likely those words of Scripture, and not someone else's commentary on those words, will stick like glue in your mind. Hearts Aflame Scripture Study is committed to this text-intensive approach. We understand that this can seem overwhelming for the beginner. In time, however, this method will prove to be worth the effort. Take heart and be patient.

⁂

"He Opened to Us the Scriptures" (Lk. 24:32)

After the introduction, you will see the above heading. It reminds us that when we read Scripture, we are seeking a conversation with the Lord in which we expect to hear Him. Before the "study" begins, we simply ask the Lord to speak to us, and then we read through the Scripture passage in the lesson. There may be much we do not understand, but that is not the concern at this point. We are looking for what we *do* understand, and based on that, we will respond very simply to the Lord. This will be a brief, initial connection that we make with Him. It happens through something that is clear to us without any further study. Why do we take the time to do this? It helps us to avoid thinking of Scripture as a text to be mastered. It is a moment of calm response to the One who can speak to us through His Word, even if we are unschooled in the Bible.

How do we make this response? Whatever it is in the passage that clearly catches our eye, we will turn into a simple prayer. Sometimes the response to God's Word can be adoration (i.e., "Lord, I adore You because of what I see about You in verse 47"). Sometimes it can be confession (i.e., "Lord, I myself have been guilty of what I see in verse 23"). Sometimes it can be joy or a desire to become more like what you observe in the passage (i.e., "O, Lord, please make me as confident in Your power and love as Saint Paul was in verse 18"). Make your response *specific*, repeating in your prayer what impressed you in the passage. There is a place in this section of the lesson for you to write out a simple response to God.

If you get stuck and cannot make a simple response after reading the passage, there is always a "prayer hint" at the very end of this section. It is placed there to make it easier for you to respond to God on your own.

❧

Questions

To assist us in the more rigorous work of studying the passage in the lesson, we have developed questions on the text. Space is provided for your responses.

We used the Revised Standard Version–Catholic Edition Bible (RSV–CE) to prepare our questions. We recommend it as the best word-for-word translation, particularly helpful for studying Scripture. However, reading the passage again in another version can also be useful.

The questions will frequently refer to the *Catechism of the Catholic Church*. You will need to have a copy for your work in this study. To study the Scripture as a Catholic is to share in the experience of the disciples on the road to Emmaus. Jesus interpreted for them the Scriptures—words that were already very familiar to them. And He continues to do that in the teaching of the Church He built. Because of her special charism of apostolic authority, the Church has two thousand years' worth of wisdom about what the Scriptures mean. Her teachings through the ages preserve the interpretive voice of Jesus. She does this by defining dogma, not by giving us a commentary on every verse in the Bible. Dogmas give us the boundaries of belief within which Scripture must be interpreted. The *Catechism* gives us access to dogmatic belief in the accumulated Tradition of the Church; it is impossible to do Catholic Bible study without it.

Some questions are fairly easy; others are not. Some of the more difficult questions are called "challenge questions." If you are unable to respond to those, don't worry. In time, you will find more and more that you are able to have a response to nearly every question. Some of the questions are designed to make you really think. You will need to read the passage over and over. *That's exactly the point!* The more you read those words, the longer they will stay with you. You have your whole life to continue this conversation with God. Do not expect to have responses to every question right away. Be patient with yourself.

❧

Guide to Lesson Questions

In the back of the book, you will find guided responses to all the questions in the lesson. In order to get the most from Hearts Aflame Scripture Study, refer to these responses only after you have answered all the questions yourself. The work you do personally on the text will stay with you longer than anything else in the lesson. Do not short-circuit the process by referring to the responses prematurely.

The responses in the back of the book are not magisterial. That is, they are not the "official" Church interpretation of the verses you are studying. They do, however, point you in an orthodox direction. They are designed to enrich your understanding of the texts you study.

☙

"Did Not Our Hearts Burn Within Us?" (Lk. 24:32)

This heading introduces the part of the study that helps us to connect what we've learned with how we live. It helps us to open the door of our souls to the Word of God. For that reason, it is possibly the most important part of the study. It recommends memorization of verses from the text as a wonderful way for God's Word to burn into our hearts. It also asks some questions that are designed for very personal reflection. Be sure to spend some quiet time with these questions. A soul opened to the light of God's Word is a soul transformed.

☙

"Stay with Us" (Lk. 24:29)

This heading reminds us that the disciples on the road to Emmaus wanted to hear *more* from Jesus after the marvelous Bible study He'd given them. They wanted to linger with Him for a while—and this led to His full revelation of Himself. The "Stay with Us" article will always be one more development of the passage you've studied, usually in a slightly new direction. We consider this part to be vital to the Hearts Aflame Scripture Study method; try hard not to think of it as optional. After you have finished the lesson, sit down in a quiet place and ponder again the beauty of God's Word. We believe you will count it worth the effort. Remember that the disciples in Emmaus fully recognized Jesus in the breaking of the bread. You, too, will need to store in your heart what you are learning from Scripture, so that when you are at Mass, you "recognize" Him in the Eucharist. Pondering the lessons is one way for you to keep the truth secure, so that the final step of recognition and transformation can take place. The "Stay with Us" article is there to help you do that.

Lesson Summary

You can use this brief summary as a checklist to make sure that you understood everything in the lesson. We have put it at the very end so it can be an easy reference for you as you start preparation on the next lesson. If some time has lapsed, you might need to be refreshed about what happened in the previous lesson as you work on the new one.

May God richly bless you as you seek Him in His Word!

Introduction

The Book of Genesis

Genesis, with its famous opening line, "In the beginning," and its well-known stories of creation and the early history of mankind, has been often trivialized and isolated from the rest of the Bible by people who don't understand its purpose, or who are convinced that modern science has relegated its stories to myth.

That is unfortunate, for the Book of Genesis does not merely tell quaint stories about people who lived at the dawn of time. The roots of all that Christians believe are found here. Read properly, Genesis reveals the essence of the nature of God, of creation, and of man. It shows how man fell from grace and God's friendship. It reveals the nature of sin. In these pages, we see the first hints of God's plan of redemption and of the promises He made, laying out the blueprint for the rest of salvation history. It is also the beginning of a very important *family* history—that of the family of God.

Genesis is first of five books that form the Pentateuch, otherwise known as the Law of Moses. The version we use dates from the time of Israel's return from Babylonian exile, around the fifth century BC. However, Jewish and Christian tradition both attribute authorship of the original draft to Moses, who wrote down what had been preserved through oral tradition or in written fragments around 1500–1400 BC. Its first eleven chapters deal with the origins of the world and mankind; the rest of the book records the action of God in creating the nation of Israel. It ends with the people of Israel living in Egypt, where they sought refuge from famine in their homeland, Canaan. Thus Genesis covers the longest time span of any book in the Bible.

Our study of Genesis is divided into two books. This is the first book, *God and His Creation*, which covers chapters 1–11, starting at the beginning of everything and continuing through the history of man, up until the call of the patriarch, Abraham—the founding father of Israel. The dramatic story of God's creation of the universe, His design and purpose for everything in it, and His response to the work of an enemy will unfold in these chapters. A second book in this Genesis series, *God and His Family*, covers the time of Abraham and the patriarchs, as told in Genesis chapters 12 to 50. The first part of this second book covers Genesis 12 to 23 and includes rich details of the life of Abraham. We will see how God worked through one human being to restore to Himself the family that was plunged into chaos as a result of disobedience in the Garden of Eden. In chapters 24 to 50, we will follow the history of Abraham's descendants, the very human family through whom God promised to eventually right all that had gone wrong in creation.

Yet it won't simply be biblical history that we learn. Through the historical details, we will encounter the infinitely tender love of God for human creatures. As we observe His relentless initiative to do whatever it takes for men to know and love Him as He originally intended, our study of Genesis will convince us that nothing will impede God's plan for His creation.

In addition, the Catholic Church has recognized that "God, the inspirer of both [Old and New] Testaments, wisely arranged that the New Testament be hidden in the Old and the Old be made manifest in the New."[1] Therefore, our study of Genesis will introduce us to *typology*. "Types" in the Old Testament are real people, places, or events that prefigure in some way the coming of Christ into human history and the redemption of the world (*Catechism*, no. 128). We will understand Jesus and the Gospel better because of our study of Genesis. We will also see how the Catholic Church has taken seriously every word of truth in this book. By her teaching and her liturgical life, the Church enables us to remain connected to God's original design for His creation. Get ready to be amazed!

---

[1] *Dei Verbum*, no. 16.

God Prepares a Home
(Genesis 1)

To Moses and those for whom he wrote, the process of creation and the scientific nature of things were shrouded in mystery too deep for man to comprehend. What was important was that God created everything, and that He made man in His image. How He went about doing it was His business, as Job was to discover (see Job 38–39).

If we approach Genesis 1 as though it is God's revelation of scientific truth, we stumble immediately upon difficulties: How was there "evening and . . . morning, one day" (v. 5) when the sun had yet to be created? How did the fruit trees grow and bear fruit before there were days and nights, or seasons? And how do we reconcile creation in six literal twenty-four-hour days, with modern geological science?

Approach Genesis 1 as divine revelation of spiritual truth, and these troubles evaporate. Genesis is more like a hymn than a treatise. It uses poetic language, with symbols and images, to relate the history of the created universe. As such, it concerns itself not with how created beings developed over time, but how they came to exist at all, and by whose decree and to what purpose. As the *Catechism of the Catholic Church* tells us, "[The first three chapters of Genesis] express in their solemn language the truths of creation—its origin and its end in God, its order and good-ness, the vocation of man, and finally the drama of sin and the hope of salvation" (*Catechism*, no. 289).

Like all good poetry, the language of the first chapters of Genesis is packed with layers of meaning. Only a slow, careful reading of them will reveal the depths and riches of truth they have to offer. We are in no hurry. We want to soak in as much as we can about who God is, what and why He created, and who we are and our purpose on earth. So let us return now to the time when time itself began.

※

"He Opened to Us the Scriptures"

Before we read God's Word, we ought to take a moment to humble ourselves before Him, remembering that His Word is primarily a conversation with us, not a textbook. "Speak, Lord, for thy servant hears" (1 Sam. 3:10) can be the prayer on our lips. Then, read all the way through Genesis 1. Think about what you understand and what you don't understand in the chapter. Make a simple response to God in terms of what you do understand. Write your prayer in this space:

_____

_____

_____

_____

_____

Now, ask for His help as you work on the questions below.
(Prayer hint: *Thank You, O Lord, for the goodness of Your creation.*")

※

Questions
Revelation about God and the Universe
※ **Read Genesis 1**

1. Genesis 1 may be very familiar to you, but do not skip this step. Read the whole chapter again out loud, noticing its poetic structure and rhythm. Go back and underline phrases that are repeated throughout the chapter.

a. What are they?

_____

_____

_____

_____

b. What do these phrases and repetitions help us to understand about God and His creation?

_____

_____

_____

_____

2. Read Genesis 1:2.

a. Who else, besides God, was present at the beginning of creation?

_____

_____

_____

b. What was He doing?

_____

_____

_____

_____

3. In verse 26, God said, "Let us make man in *our* image." What does this use of the plural suggest about God?

_____

_____

_____

_____

4. *Challenge question:* Read John 1:1–5, Colossians 1:15–18, and Hebrews 1:1–3. How do these New Testament references to the creation of the world expand the picture that we get from Genesis 1?

_____

_____

_____

_____

5. The action of Genesis 1 seems to build up to verse 26, where God says, "Let us make man in our image." Review your answer to Question 1 above. What characteristics of God would you expect man to have if he is going to be in the image and likeness of God? (See also *Catechism,* no. 357.)

_____

_____

_____

_____

6. God created man "in His own image . . . male and female" (v. 27). What does this tell us about the essential equality of male and female?

_____

_____

_____

_____

7. *Challenge question:* Note that the very first thing God did for the living creatures (v. 22) and for man and woman (v. 28) after creating them was to *bless* them. In the context of this first chapter of Genesis, what did it mean for man and beast to have God's *blessing*?

_____

_____

_____

_____

8. God gave man a charge to obey as well as a blessing (v. 28).
a. How did the charge given to man differ from that given to the animals?

_____

_____

_____

_____

b. God told man to be fruitful and to have dominion over the earth. How do these two commands that God gave to man confirm that he was indeed made in the image and likeness of God?

_____

_____

_____

_____

"Lights in the Firmament of the Heavens" (Gen. 1:14)

In verse 16, "God made the two great lights, the greater light to rule the day, and the lesser light to rule the night." Note that the sun and moon are not named. In the ancient world, the very words "sun" and "moon" were synonymous with the names of deities. In contrast, Genesis teaches that the sun and moon are not powers to be feared, but created things with a God-given purpose in the universe. They were put in dominion over day and night. These lights in the firmament are the only elements in creation, besides man, that have dominion. They "rule" over the night and day, but they have no jurisdiction over man or the earth. Psalm 19 tells us of another function they serve—to tell the glory of God. When we gaze at them, we should recognize the power and beauty of God who made them.

The text says these lights (sun, moon, stars) are to serve as "signs" and to mark out time and seasons. What might they be signs of? Think of the star that the magi followed to find the newborn King in Bethlehem. Think also of the eclipse of the sun on Good Friday. God uses these elements to communicate with His creation. Think also about the description of Mary that we see in Revelation 12:1: "And a great portent appeared in the heaven, a woman clothed with the sun, with the moon under her feet, and on her head a garland of twelve stars." Is it any wonder that the Church understands Mary to be the Queen of Heaven, since, in this heavenly vision, she wears as garments the elements of dominion that we first meet in Genesis?

9. After blessing man and the animals and giving them their responsibilities, God gave gifts to them all.
a. What gifts did God give them (vv. 29–30)?

_____

_____

_____

_____

b. What kind of relationship between God and His creation did this provision establish?

_____

_____

_____

_____

10. God, perfect in Himself, needs nothing to make Him complete or happy. As you read through Genesis 1, what appears to have been God's motivation in bringing the universe into existence? Read especially verse 31.

_____

_____

_____

Timelessness

If God created time and space, as we see here in Genesis 1, He lives outside of them. It is a difficult concept to comprehend, isn't it? And yet Catholic life is pervaded with an element of "timelessness." That is because Catholic piety and liturgical life are deeply rooted in "remembering," an action that is as close to timelessness as humans can get. Because our minds make memories, some things that happened in the past are still alive to us. God built His relationship with His people, Israel, on the foundation of the human mind's ability to remember. For example, from the time of the Passover, when God delivered His people from slavery in Egypt, He commanded them to continually "remember" His great works on their behalf. This was not just a pious recollection of their departure from Egypt. It involved offering up a sacrifice of a lamb every year at the same time the deliverance had occurred, although the blood of the lamb was not painted on the doors again. A festal meal of the sacrificed lamb would follow, in which each element would make present again for the partakers the circumstances of that wonderful night of deliverance. This memorial erased the boundaries of time. It was as if, for all Israelites, time had stood still.

Catholic life enables us to experience this very same thing—timelessness— every time we go to Mass. We understand that, during the Liturgy of the Eucharist, the sacrifice of Jesus, made once for all on Calvary and offered continually before the throne of God in heaven, is made present to us sacramentally. At that point, we are not bound by time or space. In this moment of intense communion with God, it is entirely appropriate that we, mortals though we are, encounter Him in a way that is outside of time and space, since we can see from Genesis 1 that He dwells outside of them. Likewise, in our liturgical calendar and in many of our pious works (praying the Rosary, doing the Stations of the Cross, etc.), we are continually revisiting episodes in the life of Jesus, blinking past all the years that separate us in time from them. As Catholics, we are blessed to have many experiences of the eternal Now.

≋
"Did Not Our Hearts Burn?"

Our hearts will burn with joy when we consciously open them wide to God's Word. Scripture memorization is a good way to get that started. Here is a suggested memory verse:

In the beginning God created the heavens and the earth. . . . And God saw everything that he had made, and behold, it was very good.

—*Gen. 1:1, 31*

Continue to welcome Him into your soul by reflecting on these questions:

From the dawn of human history, men have marveled over the beauty and majesty of the creation, and the God from whom it comes. Read, as a prayer, Psalm 104. Join your voice to the ceaseless praise of the power and greatness of God, which rises up from the work of His hands.

_____
_____
_____
_____
_____

For some of us, to "subdue the earth" means washing a pile of dirty dishes or changing the oil in a car. These are actions we take in order for life as we know it to be maintained on the planet. Think of what you will do this day to "subdue" the earth. How can knowing that you are living out your God-given calling make a difference in the way you do that work?

_____
_____
_____
_____

≋
"Stay with Us"

Reading the first chapter of Genesis is an experience different from reading any other passage of Scripture. Think about the significance of the fact that the beginning of our human story is told in poetic language. As Joseph Cardinal Ratzinger has written, "These words, with which Holy Scripture begins, always have the effect on me of the solemn tolling of a great old bell, which stirs the heart from afar with its beauty and dignity and gives it an inkling of the mystery of eternity."[1] Just as human poetry

---

[1] Joseph Cardinal Ratzinger, *In the Beginning: A Catholic Understanding of the Story of Creation and the Fall,* trans. Boniface Ramsey (Huntington, IN: Our Sunday Visitor, 1990), 11.

seeks to take the reader beyond the limits of ordinary language to a place of exquisite meaning, so this account in Genesis communicates to us something far more than science or chronological historical narrative could ever do. By the time we've read it all the way through, we find ourselves in a kind of beatitude. We are surrounded by the goodness of God in His creation, reflected in His careful ordering of all its elements and represented most clearly in His blessing of that which breathes the breath of life. The universe exists today through the imagination, power, and love of God. Genesis 1 convinces us that no other explanation fits all the data.

Yet the details of this chapter go beyond even that. They give us our first clues about the unique relationship that exists between God and man, the "crown of creation," as the psalmist calls him. We recognized that in the action of the Blessed Trinity during creation, there was an intimation of a splendid communion within God. And as the verses in the chapter continued in their cadence, we discovered that man was to be included in this communion ("let us make man"). We saw that man, male and female, was made in the image and likeness of God, reflecting God's own nature in the vocation of fruitfulness and dominion. By sharing His image with man and imparting to him His goodness, God made clear that this communion is one of love. Only love can explain the condescension of God to man. Only love will qualify as the appropriate response to it.

Lesson Summary

✔ Genesis 1 is far more than an account of our beginnings. It is the introduction to God's written revelation of Himself, and as such, it introduces us to God, the awesome, powerful Creator of the universe. It illustrates the power of His Word, the goodness of all of His works, and the deliberate, orderly intent behind His creativity. It shows Him to be the only, eternal, omnipresent source of life, and of all that is needed to sustain it. Together with His Word and Spirit, He creates and sustains all by His will and by His love.

✔ God's created universe is altogether good and perfect and well-ordered. In its beauty and splendor, goodness, order and infinite variety, it reflects the One who made it. Each piece reflects a different aspect of the Creator and together gloriously reflects the whole. The universe is designed as a great household, a habitation for an enormous variety of life, ruled over by God's crowning creature, mankind.

✔ Man and woman were created in God's image and endowed with His very life. Mankind is thus set apart in a unique way from the rest of creation. The image of God in man means that he has a will and can act freely. He is able to reason, to create, and to appreciate goodness. He has a capacity for eternal life, since the God whom he reflects dwells outside of time. In his vocation, which is to be fruitful and exercise dominion over the earth, he carries on the work of God begun in creation. God's delight, satisfaction, and pleasure in man are verified by His blessing. Every single human being can look at Genesis 1 to comprehend his place and meaning in the universe.

For responses to Lesson 1 Questions, see pp. 105–7.

God Creates a Family
(Genesis 2)

In Genesis 1, we saw God speak the universe into existence, then form it into a house, or habitation. He filled it with life by the power of His Word. With help from the New Testament, we understood that the creation of the natural order was a work of the Blessed Trinity. It culminated in the presence of man and woman on earth—creatures made in the image of God and reflecting Him in their vocation to fruitfulness and dominion. The poetic language of that chapter was itself a sign that God's purposes for His creation, most especially for the creatures who would be His presence on earth, cannot be exhaustively described by words. Poetry moves beyond the words it uses.

The words of Genesis 1 were just a hint of the glory that lies at the heart of creation. By the end of that chapter, all that was contained in it throbbed with the love of God—an ecstasy of goodness.

In Genesis 2, the focus of the story will be on the human creatures. Having watched God build a home for them in the previous chapter, now we will observe more closely the creation of Adam and Eve, their relationship with God and with each other. In fact, Genesis 2 is where we begin to see that God is not simply "Master of the Universe" or "Creator." His intention for His creation was always that it would exist with Him as His family. Male and female were made in His "image and likeness," (children are always in the likeness of their parents). Like a good Father, God looked after every need of man. And as a wise Father, He set boundaries for them to enjoy a safe and happy life. In addition, He established a human relationship, marriage, which would reflect the mystery and joy of His own nature—the communion of the Blessed Trinity. Thus begins the story of the family of God.

❧

"He Opened to Us the Scriptures"

Before we read God's Word, we ought to take a moment to humble ourselves before Him, remembering that His Word is primarily a conversation with us, not a textbook. "Speak, Lord, for thy servant hears" (1 Sam. 3:10) can be the prayer on our lips. Then, read all the way through Genesis 2. Think about what you understand and what you don't understand. Make a simple response to God in terms of what you do understand. Write your prayer in this space:

_____

_____

_____

_____

_____

Now, ask for His help as you work on the questions below.
(Prayer hint: *Thank You, O Lord, that You fill the deepest needs of Your creatures.*)

❧

Questions
Completion and Rest: The Seventh Day
❧ **Read Gen. 2:1–3**

1. We see that God rested on the seventh day, after six days of creative work. Surely this wasn't because He was worn out by the work. Why do you think He rested?

_____

_____

_____

_____

The First Covenant

If we were reading Genesis 2 in Hebrew, verse 3 would almost sound like God finished His work and rested on the "oath" day, and blessed the "oath" day and hallowed it. The word, translated as "seven" in our English text, is the Hebrew word (*sheba*) for "oath-sharing." When men in ancient times came together to form a relationship in which they would treat each other as family, they swore an oath to seal the agreement. In Hebrew, "to swear an oath" means literally "to seven oneself." This kind of agreement is called a "covenant." In contrast to a contract, in which there is an exchange of property, a covenant involves an exchange of persons: "I am yours, you are mine." It is possible that to the ancient Hebrews, God's rest on the seventh day meant that He had formed a covenant, or sworn an oath, with all the elements of creation, establishing a family relationship with them. That would have bestowed a kind of animation even on what was inanimate. For example, in Genesis 2:4, the text reads, "These are the gener-

12

ations of the heavens and the earth when they were created." The word "generations" usually refers to living things. Likewise, in Psalms 148, the heavens and the deep, sun and stars, snow and hills, sea monsters and cattle—*all* creation sings out in praise to the Lord who created them. If God formed a covenant with all creation by resting on the "oath" day, then all creation is filled with God's glory and is part of His household.

The Creation of Man

✣ Read Gen. 2:4–7

*[**Note:** Up until now, the Creator has been referred to as "God" (*Elohim *in Hebrew, meaning "Master"). Beginning in 2:4, He is called "L*ORD *God," or "Yahweh." This was the personal, covenant name of God used by the people of Israel. It signals a transition in the account from details about the creation of the cosmos to the intimate relationship of God with man.]*

2. The real focus of this chapter is the formation of man. Review 1:20, 24, 26–27 along with 2:7, 18–19.

   a. How was the creation of man different from the creation of the animals?

_____
_____
_____
_____

   b. Read the *Catechism,* nos. 363 and 366. What are the implications of the breath of God in man?

_____
_____
_____
_____

The Creation of the Garden

✣ Read Gen. 2:8–17

*[**Note:** If we read this chapter in terms of God establishing a covenant with those created to be his children, this section can be seen as containing the terms or conditions of the covenant at this early stage: the blessing of eternal life with God would be preserved by obedience to a prohibition or lost through disobedience.]*

3. Read the description of the place God set apart and prepared for man to live in verse 9.

   a. Describe it.

_____
_____
_____
_____
_____

b. Why do you think the Garden was sensuously beautiful, in addition to being functional?

_____

_____

_____

_____

c. *Challenge question:* If, at creation, the place on earth where God communed with man was full of beauty, what might we expect to be characteristic of all other places on earth where God communes with man?

_____

_____

_____

4. The Hebrew word for "keep" in verse 15 is better translated "guard." If you had been Adam, hearing the charge from God to guard the Garden, what question might it have provoked in you?

_____

_____

_____

_____

5. *Challenge question:* Look at verses 16–17. Why would a loving God, whom we just saw carefully create all things "good" and make a beautiful dwelling place for His children, put a desirable but deadly and forbidden tree in the middle of the Garden? (Read also *Catechism,* no. 396.)

_____

_____

_____

_____

Sanctified Time and Sanctified Space

When the world began, God marked out one day from the others as holy. In other words, He sanctified time. The Church continues to sanctify time as God did in creation, and as the Jews did in their life as His people. Their first experience of sanctified time came in the desert, after they had been delivered from the bondage of slavery in Egypt. Even before God gave the Ten Commandments to Moses at Mount Sinai, He told the people to keep a Sabbath rest (see Ex. 16:23) to commemorate their deliverance. Catholic Christians continue to mark out time as holy by the observance of the Lord's day, Sunday, as well as other days and seasons of special importance in the liturgical calendar. Our holy days of obligation are perpetual reminders of the good things God has done on our behalf. We use time itself to honor Him.

Notice, also, that verse 8 says that the Lord God put the man He had formed in a special place on the earth—a garden in the east, called Eden. Just as God had done with time, setting aside one hallowed day, so He did with space as well. He set aside one place on all the earth for man to live. This would be the place where God and man communed in a unique and intimate way. It was holy space. God is Spirit, so He is omnipresent. He is everywhere. Yet from the beginning, it has been His desire to be near to His people in their human lives, within the boundaries of time and space. The Garden of Eden was just such a place. This is seen most clearly, perhaps, in the next chapter, where the text tells us that God was "walking in the Garden in the cool of the day" (Gen. 3:8). This is not to say that He was in the form of a man there, but that His presence and accessibility to Adam and Eve were like what one experiences during a conversation on a pleasant walk. When this "holy space" was lost through disobedience, God restored it first in the "holy of holies." That was the special place, in both the tabernacle (the tent where Israel worshiped God during their desert wanderings, after their escape from Egypt) and the Temple in Jerusalem, where God met with Israel's High Priest. The full restoration of communion between God and man took place in Jesus, when "the Word became flesh and dwelt among us" (Jn. 1:14). Forever after that, until He returns, Jesus makes Himself present and accessible in that flesh to humans in the Sacrament of the Eucharist. The red tabernacle lamps in our churches are the sign that, just as in the Garden, we are standing in "holy space."

The Creation of Eve
🎜 **Read Gen. 2:18–25**

6. Being alone was the first thing pronounced "not good" (v. 18) in the account of creation.

    a. Why do you think that was so? (Hint: Go back and review 1:26–27.)

_____

_____

_____

_____

    b. Why do you think God intended to make a "helper" and not simply a companion for the man?

_____

_____

_____

_____

7. Surely God did not expect that one of the beasts of the field would be a fit helper for Adam. So what do you think explains this episode of Adam and the animals?

_____

_____

_____

_____

8. What do you suppose is the significance of the Lord God creating woman from Adam's rib, instead of simply forming her from the dust of the ground?

_____

_____

_____

_____

9. Look at Adam's response to the creation of Eve in verse 23.
   a. Why do you think Adam was so delighted with the appearance of Eve?

_____

_____

_____

_____

b. See that Adam's delight in Eve, described in verse 23, is followed by a description of marriage in verse 24. In marriage, husband and wife "cleave" to each other and become "one flesh." What does this suggest to us about the purpose of marriage? (See also *Catechism,* nos. 1603–5.)

_____

_____

_____

_____

c. If marriage creates "one flesh," of which offspring are living signs, what does that suggest about divorce? Read also Matthew 19:1–6. (See also *Catechism,* nos. 1646–51.)

_____

_____

_____

_____

[Note: We can see that God gave to husband and wife the work He had begun of creating human life. From that moment to this, human life on earth was to be the result of sexual union, a divine act between husband and wife (see Catechism, *no. 2367).]*

Human Sexuality "in the Beginning"
God created Adam from the dust of the ground and breathed the breath of life into him (see Gen. 2:7). The Hebrew word for "breath" in the original language is also a word for "spirit." And let's remember that the Spirit of God is the very love between the Father and the Son. God is breathing *His love* into the man.

What this means . . . is that the man is a person called to live in a relationship of love with God. The man, having received the love of God, is called to give himself back to God. He's also called to share the love of God with others (see Mt. 22:37–40). It's stamped in his very being, and he can only fulfill himself by doing so. As the Second Vatican Council put it, "Man, who is the only creature on earth that God created for his own sake, cannot fully find himself except through the sincere gift of himself."

This is why the Lord said, "It is not good that the man should be alone; I will make him a helper fit for him" (Gen. 2:18). That is, God said, "I will make someone he can love.". . .

So the Lord put the man into a deep sleep and took a rib from his side. . . . "Deep sleep" might better be translated "ecstasy." Ecstasy literally means "to go out of oneself," and Adam's "ecstasy" is that God takes a woman *out of himself.* Furthermore, in the original language, the word "rib" is a play on the word "life." That's to say, the woman comes from the very same *life* as the man. . . .

Now imagine Adam's state of mind when he awoke to the sight of the woman. The deepest desire of his heart is to give himself away in love to another person "like himself," and he has just finished naming billions of animals and found no one. So what does he say?

"At last, you are the one! You are bone of my bone and flesh of my flesh" (see Gen. 2:23). That is, "At last, a person like myself that I can love."

How does Adam know that she's the one he can love? Remember that they were naked. It was their *bodies* that revealed the spiritual truth of the persons. In their nakedness they discovered what John Paul II calls the "nuptial meaning of the body," that is, "the [body's] capacity of expressing love: that love precisely in which the person becomes a gift and—by means of this gift—fulfills the very meaning of his being and existence."

Adam looked at himself; he looked at Eve. He realized this profound reality: "We go together. God made us *for* each other. I can give myself to you, and you can give yourself to me, and we can live in a life-giving communion of love"—the image of God, marriage.

That was the sentiment of sexual desire as God created it and as they experienced it: to make a gift of themselves to each other in the image of God. This is why they were naked and felt no shame (see Gen. 2:25). There's no shame in loving as God loves, only the experience of joy, peace, and a deep knowledge of human goodness.[1]

---

[1] Reprinted from Christopher West, *Good News About Sex and Marriage* (Ann Arbor, MI: Servant Publications, 2000), 18–19.

10. *Challenge question:* The context of Genesis 2 helps us to understand the meaning, or purpose, of marriage. Why is the Church's teaching that "it is necessary that each and every marriage act remain ordered *per se* to the procreation of human life" (*Catechism,* no. 2366, quoting *Humanae Vitae* no. 11)) entirely consistent with what we see in Genesis 2?

_____

_____

_____

_____

✣

"Did Not Our Hearts Burn Within Us?"

Our hearts will burn with joy when we consciously open them wide to God's Word. Scripture memorization is a good way to get that started. Here is a suggested memory verse:

And the man and his wife were both naked, and were not ashamed.

—Gen. 2:25

Continue to welcome Him into your soul by reflecting on these questions:

The Church calls us to hallow time by holy days of obligation, most especially the Lord's Day. In addition, each day offers us an opportunity to hallow time by offering some of it back to God in rest and worship of Him. Have you established this habit, sometimes referred to as keeping a "holy hour"? If not, reflect on the importance of hallowed time that Genesis 2 reveals. Consider imitating God by hallowing one hour out of twenty-four, saving that one for Him and Him alone.

_____

_____

_____

Because each of us is either male or female, reading Genesis 2 enables us to see the uniqueness of our own sexual identity as we observe the design and purposes for each sex. Take time to reflect on your place in God's plan as male or female. Whether you are single or married, is there anything in today's lesson that will enable you to be a better man or woman of God?

_____

_____

_____

The choice put before Adam and Eve, and represented by the trees of life and of death, echoes throughout Scripture and throughout our lives. It is the choice to obey

God and to live as He has asked us to live. Think about the choices you face in each day of your life. Choices become habits. Ask God to give you the grace to examine your habits to see if you are choosing wisely.

_____

_____

_____

_____

❧

"Stay with Us"

In the careful, patient narrative of Genesis 2, we have had the opportunity to gaze at the "picture" of man and woman in Paradise. What do we see?

The creation of man catches our eye because, in it, we recognize his difference from everything else in the universe. He is made from the dust of the ground, but God breathes His own life into him. He is of earth, but he is also spiritual. Because of his two-fold nature, all the other details of Genesis 2 will expand his identity in one direction or the other. He is sensual, so he is surrounded by great physical beauty. He gets hungry, so he is provided with food. He gets lonely, so a helper is created for him. He has a body of which he is not ashamed.

He is not, however, a creature like the other animals. He is made in the image of God, so there is much more we need to know about him to understand him. As God creates life, so will man be able to cooperate in procreation. As God worked to bring the universe into existence, man will work to care for it. As God is free in Himself, so man is free in himself to choose his destiny. As God is a communion of equals, so will man be, with the creation of woman.

If we had to describe this scene, what words would we use? Although the word "love" never appears in the text, can we have any doubt that under and over and through it all, the love of God permeates every detail? Can we not feel the delight of God in these blessed creatures? Are we not moved to smile at the deep joy of human communion expressed in the first encounter of Adam and Eve? Although Adam came from the dust of the ground, does not the breath of God in him bestow on him unsurpassable dignity in this scene? And does not his helper, Eve, drawn from his side, share that dignity as she completes the image of God in them, male and female?

Be sure you take the time to rest in this scene and drink in deep draughts of the air that is heavy with blessedness here. Try to picture the sensuous beauty of the Garden—the sight and smell of the beautiful fruit trees, the sound and feel of rushing water in the four rivers that flow out from it, the taste of the Tree of Life. See Adam and Eve, ready to begin their family as man and wife. Let the tranquility and harmony of this chapter sink deeply into your imagination and soul. It shouldn't take too long for you to realize that Paradise is not only home for Adam and Eve. It is your own true home as well.

Lesson Summary

✔ As the narrator moved from the grand strokes of creation, which we saw in Genesis 1, to focus on the creation of man, he no longer called God *"Elohim"* (Master of the Universe), but *"Yahweh"* (Lord God)—Israel's personal, covenant name for God. God completed His work on the sixth day and rested on the seventh, establishing a covenant with all creation and blessing it.

✔ God created man in His own image and likeness, endowing him with a dignity above all other created beings. He then made from Adam a helper, Eve, to co-labor with him. Only together as male and female, and as a communion of equals, did they fully reflect God's image. All people can trace their lineage back to the same first parents and, thus, share equally in the dignity of the same family.

✔ God formed and set apart a place of blessing and beauty where man was to live in fellowship with Him. Man was given the job of tilling and keeping (or guarding) the Garden. In this work, he was not a slave but a collaborator with God in perfecting creation.

✔ In the Garden, man was offered eternal life with God, but he was also given the choice, in the form of a prohibition, of refusing that life. Thus, man's covenant family relationship with God would be preserved through obedience.

✔ Although Adam and Eve had knowledge of good and evil, the prerogative of deciding what was good or evil belonged to God.

✔ Not only was woman made from man, she (as his wife) was made to once again become "one flesh" with him in marriage. They would become, as husband and wife, a new, indivisible creation, both in their marriage union and in their offspring. In innocence and freedom, they were naked and not ashamed.

For responses to Lesson 2 Questions, see pp. 108–10.

Temptation and Fall
(Genesis 3:1-6)

In our study of Genesis, we are now approaching the moment when human history took a dramatic turn. It will be important for us to take in and consider carefully every detail. For two chapters, we have been enthralled with what we have seen of God's power, creativity, and love. We have had a growing understanding of God and man. We have seen that God hallowed time and space. He provided for every need His creatures had—both their physical and spiritual appetites. For their bodies, God supplied food and water most abundantly. For their souls, the breath of God in them, He gave them the work of dominion and procreation, reflecting His own life. As male and female, they would share a communion of equals. They would be free to choose to love God, as He freely chose to create and love them. We observed in the Garden that man had a mind with which to think (he recognized that the animals were not his equals), a will with which to choose, and senses to experience his physical life. For his mind, God gave man truth—what he needed to *know* in order to live. For his will, God gave man a choice between good and evil—what he needed to *do* in order to live. For his senses, God put man in the midst of great beauty, so that the visible world would bear testimony to him of the goodness and wisdom of the invisible God. The life God gave to man and woman in the Garden was perfectly suited to His design for them. The tranquility, harmony, and innocence there resulted from all things being exactly how God intended them.

It didn't last. Now we must brace ourselves to understand what happened next. We will need to slow down even more than our leisurely pace through the first two chapters. We don't want familiarity with this part of the story to rob us of its importance. In this lesson, we will examine the test that Adam and Eve underwent. Did we see it coming? Are we shocked at its severity? Are we incredulous that man succumbed? What really lies at the heart of the human story if it begins with such a catastrophic failure? If reading the first two chapters of Genesis was a time for long, appreciative sighs, reading chapter three will be a time for questions, questions, and more questions.

Genesis 3 will be divided into three sections. This lesson will examine the temptation and Fall. The next two will deal with the consequences.

❦

"He Opened to Us the Scriptures"

Before we read God's Word, we ought to take a moment to humble ourselves before Him, remembering that His Word is primarily a conversation with us, not a textbook. "Speak, Lord, for thy servant hears" (1 Sam. 3:10) can be the prayer on our lips. Then, read all the way through Genesis 3:1–6. Think about what you understand and what you don't understand. Make a simple response to God in terms of what you do understand. Write your prayer in this space:

_____

_____

_____

_____

Now, ask for His help as you work on the questions below.
(Prayer hint: *"Lord, deliver me from evil when it stalks me."*)

❦

Questions
The Challenge

❦ **Read Gen. 3:1–3**

1. Storybooks portray the serpent in the Garden almost as a cartoon character. Read Revelation 12:3–9 and 20:2 to see how the Bible describes him outside of Genesis. Who was the serpent? (Read also *Catechism,* no. 391–95.)

_____

_____

_____

_____

"A Seductive Voice, Opposed to God" (*Catechism,* no. 391)

One of the most unsettling elements in this scene of temptation in Genesis 3 is the sudden appearance of an enemy of God. We wonder, "Where did he come from?" If we read back over the details of Genesis 1 and 2, we do not find a single clue to help us answer this question. We are left with the obvious but unsatisfying conclusion that the story recorded in Genesis is our story but not the whole story of God and His creation. When our story gets underway, we find that there was another story of rebellion against God, the details of which we only know in barest outline. This is humbling, of course, because we want to know everything. We can, at this point, become bitter and demand more information. Or, we can do a truly human thing, which is to accept our limitations. Perhaps reading on in the story here will help us make our choice.

2. It is surprising to see that the serpent entered the tranquility of the Garden.
  a. What question does this serpent's appearance provoke?

_____

_____

_____

_____

  b. *Challenge question:* Everything that we have seen about God in Genesis thus far revealed Him to be good, loving, and wise. Because of that, what can we say with confidence about the presence of the serpent in the Garden? (Read also *Catechism,* nos. 309–14.)

_____

_____

_____

_____

3. The serpent began speaking to the woman.
  a. Why do you think he addressed himself to the woman instead of to Adam, who was in charge of the Garden (Gen. 2:15)?

_____

_____

_____

_____

  b. Where do you suppose Adam was?

_____

_____

_____

_____

4. The end of verse 1 is best translated, "Did God say, 'You shall not eat of *every* tree of the garden?'"
  a. Read what God actually said to Adam in Genesis 2:16–17. How did the serpent change the wording of the commandment?

_____

_____

_____

_____

b. What suspicion about God did the serpent's rephrasing of the command imply?

_____
_____
_____
_____

5. Look at the woman's answer in verses 2–3. Why do you suppose she added a prohibition against even touching the tree, which was not there in the original command?

_____
_____
_____
_____

The Deception

𝄞 **Read Gen. 3:4–5**

6. Look carefully at the enticement to eat the fruit that the serpent made to the woman in verses 4–5.

a. How much of the "benefit" of eating the fruit did the man and woman already possess, without having to eat the fruit?

_____
_____
_____
_____

b. What did the serpent insinuate about God's character in his appeal to the woman?

_____
_____
_____
_____

c. *Challenge question:* If the serpent wasn't offering anything new to the man and woman, what was the real nature of his temptation?

_____
_____
_____
_____

7. The serpent maligned God's character and deceived the woman.

a. What should Adam have done at this point in the story?

_____
_____
_____
_____

b. Why do you suppose he was silent?

_____
_____
_____
_____

c. What were the consequences of Adam's silence and passivity?

_____
_____
_____
_____

The Decision

🗲 **Read Gen. 3:6**

8. After hearing the serpent's pitch, the woman fixed her focus on the tree.
a. What was it about the tree that she found so appealing?

_____
_____
_____
_____

b. What should these characteristics of the tree have done to help the woman obey God?

_____
_____
_____
_____

c. *Challenge question:* Read 1 John 2:15–17. How do you think the tree's appearance led the woman into disobedience?

_____
_____
_____
_____

9. This was a severe test of the man and the woman. Because of its familiarity to us, we can easily forget that it didn't have to turn out the way it did.
a. What did the man and the woman know about God and themselves that should have given them the strength to resist the serpent's temptation?

_____
_____
_____
_____

b. In the moment of temptation, the man and the woman did not see God. They only saw the serpent, the tree, and each other. What should their knowledge of God have enabled them to do? (Read also Heb. 11:1–2, 6; 2 Cor. 4:17–18.)

_____

_____

_____

_____

≋

"Did Not Our Hearts Burn Within Us?"

Our hearts will burn with joy when we consciously open them wide to God's Word. Scripture memorization is a good way to get that started. Here is a suggested memory verse:

> *So when the woman saw that the tree was good for food, and that it was a delight to the eyes, and that the tree was to be desired to make one wise, she took of its fruit and ate; and she also gave some to her husband, and he ate.*
>
> *—Gen. 3:6*

Continue to welcome Him into your soul by reflecting on these questions:

Notice how crafty the serpent was in the way he tempted the woman. He began by questioning God's simple commandment. Then he carefully distorted it, by means of half-truths, so that ultimately he attacked God's character. Paraphrased, it might read something like this: "God *pretends* to love you, but He has put a severe limitation on your freedom. He can't be trusted, you know. He doesn't really like you very much." Are there places in your life in which you are subject to this kind of temptation? Be specific. What has this lesson done to strengthen you against it?

_____

_____

_____

_____

In order to pass the test in the Garden, the man and the woman needed to live by faith, trusting in God, whom they could not see. What is the hardest part of having to live by faith in your life right now? As you think over the details of where your faith is weak and struggling against the appearance of things, use this prayer of a man in the Gospels to find strength: "Lord, I believe; help my unbelief!" (Mk. 9:24).

_____

_____

_____

❦
"Stay with Us"

Was it painful to watch the slow descent of our first parents from their place of dignity and grace in the Garden to their willingness to obey the voice of a traitor? Perhaps you had the impulse to cry out, "Stop the action! Don't make another move!" No matter how many times we read it, our hearts grow heavy with the weight of what Adam and Eve had and lost. Made in God's image and given everything they needed for a happy, blessed life, they "exchanged the truth about God for a lie" (Rom. 1:25). They abused their freedom to declare their autonomy from Him, if not by words, then by their actions. God put them to the test, and they failed miserably.

In this chapter, we learned that God has an enemy. The fallen angel, whom we call Satan, made his first appearance in Genesis, and, although he was only on the stage briefly, we saw him for exactly what he is. He hates God and God's creatures. His rebellion against God, for whatever reason, filled him with contempt for human beings. He taunted them with their dependence on God. He attacked the character of God, both His credibility and His goodness. He lured their focus away from the good God, who created the world (and who should be obeyed for that reason), to the good thing God had created in the forbidden fruit. He convinced the humans that, while God may have had some valuable ideas about what constitutes good and evil, they could and should gain that kind of knowledge on their own.

What an irony it is that the key player in this scene is the one from whom we hear nothing. Adam was the one who could have put an end to this insurrection. He had been put in charge of the Garden, and he knew that God had said that eating the forbidden fruit would kill them. He had firsthand experience of the kindness, goodness, and wisdom of God when he was lonely and in need of a helper. By His Word and by His actions, God had revealed Himself to be devoted to the happiness and well-being of His creatures. Yet when the serpent appeared and began his conversation with the woman, Adam remained silent. He made no attempt to fight for God's honor or to protect his bride from villainy. Had he trusted God, he would have done whatever it took to cast off this attack. Instead, he listened to the voice of the serpent and then to the voice of his wife. Is this really the creature made in God's image, into whom God had breathed His own breath?

The woman weighed the benefits of acting independently of God. She seemed to have much to gain by throwing off the restraint God had placed on the forbidden fruit. In the face of Adam's silence, did she feel any shame before the serpent for looking so gullible, so willing to just accept God's prohibition about the fruit? She was the only one left in the Garden who still believed God's Word. Did she talk herself into doing what she knew was wrong just to save face?

It takes an effort, doesn't it, to force ourselves to stop asking questions. How we'd love to get to the bottom of this disaster. Surely that comes from a deep impulse inside of us to undo all the wrong and to make it all right. How we long to rewrite this story! Perhaps that is because we sense intuitively what the Church teaches us explicitly: we are not dispassionate observers of this scene. By the choice of Adam and Eve to disobey God, they lost original justice and became wounded in their natures (as we will see in the next lesson). Human nature is passed on through procreation. If these two humans are allowed to live and procreate, every human being born into the world will bear that same wounded nature (see *Catechism,* nos. 403–7). But lest we despair, we need to take a step back and remember that this is actually the *beginning* of our story. What can it mean that our story starts with a failure? Is it too much to hope that the only way out is up?

Lesson Summary

✔ The glorious relationship that existed between God and His human creatures, so clearly set forth in the first two chapters of Genesis, is revealed in chapter three to have been rooted in freedom. As God was free, so were His creatures. The life He designed for them depended on their cooperation. Obedience would enable them to fulfill their destiny; disobedience would bring death.

✔ Man's love for God, in order to be free and genuine, had to be tested. The devil, a fallen angel who had rebelled against God and refused to serve Him, was allowed to enter the Garden to tempt Adam and Eve. He appeared as a usurper, contradicting God and presenting himself as one with greater knowledge and more interest in the creatures' well-being than God. Through cunning deception, he disguised the gifts from God already in the possession of the man and woman; he made them appear as enticing new possibilities that could only be gained through disobedience.

✔ Adam, whose responsibility it was to guard the Garden and his bride, silently stood by and did nothing. His trust in God died. He was not willing to suffer whatever might have been required of him to oppose the serpent. He did not even cry out for help.

✔ Without anyone to counter the serpent's insinuations, and perhaps believing that, by his silence, Adam had already given up on God, the woman turned her attention to the visible realities before her, forgetting the invisible ones. If Adam counted God's Word for nothing, why should she still foolishly cling to it? She ate the fruit, which had a tremendous appeal to her. And instead of Adam leading her away from danger, he followed her into the heart of it.

For responses to Lesson 3 Questions, see pp. 111–15.

A Curse and a Promise
(Genesis 3:7–15)

It is a grim scene indeed in which the only glimmer of hope is that things can't get any worse. Yet we allowed ourselves to be consoled by that thought in our last lesson. The human story crashed into failure and loss. Adam and Eve were faced with a choice about how they would live. Their freedom to choose God or reject Him was what made them truly human—different from the beasts and in the image of God. Once the serpent appeared on the scene, we knew that their choice was to be made under difficult circumstances. Although they could not see God, they had His Word of commandment and many evidences of His goodness. The visible serpent and the easily observed appeal of the forbidden fruit were challenges to them, but they could have counted the invisible truth as the one that mattered most. Had Adam believed God and acted on that trust, he would have thrown himself into combating the interloper, even if it meant suffering. Love of God would have made Adam willing to do whatever it required to protect God's name, his bride, and the Garden. But Adam chose self-love. The rest is history.

If there were no *hope* in this history, it would have ended there. God might simply have blotted everything out and started over again, much like a cook disposes of a first batch of cookies that got burnt. That the story continues *at all* means hope, even if it is only modest. As we move on through the rest of the details of Genesis 3, we want to be on the look out for more signs of hope. This is going to take a special kind of eyesight, however, because immediately after the Fall, the light in the Garden started to dim. There was the chill of a dark shadow casting itself over what was once luminous in its glory and perfection. How will the human creatures be different? What will they say to God? What will He say to them? And, for the really burning question, what will He *do* to them? The answers to these questions will occupy us for the next two lessons.

❧

"He Opened to Us the Scriptures"

Before we read God's Word, we ought to take a moment to humble ourselves before Him, remembering that His Word is primarily a conversation with us, not a textbook. "Speak, Lord, for thy servant hears" (1 Sam. 3:10) can be the prayer on our lips. Then, read all the way through Genesis 3:7–15. Think about what you understand and what you don't understand. Make a simple response to God in terms of what you do understand. Write your prayer in this space:

_____

_____

_____

_____

_____

Now, ask for His help as you work on the questions below.
(Prayer hint: *"Lord, heal my sin that makes me blind."*)

❧

Questions
Discovery and Effect

❧ **Read Gen. 3:7–13**

1. Review Genesis 3:1–6. The serpent had promised the woman that if she ate the fruit, her eyes would be opened. That was exactly what happened (v. 7).
a. We know that the man and woman saw each other naked and were not ashamed before their disobedience (Gen. 2:25). After the Fall, they wanted to cover up their nakedness, even though their bodies hadn't changed. What were their eyes "opened" to see that they hadn't seen before? (Read also *Catechism*, nos. 399–400.)

_____

_____

_____

b. What was the second effect of their disobedience (v. 8)?

_____

_____

_____

Original Sin

The obvious systemic change that took place in Adam and Eve because of their disobedience was a radical change in human nature, which they have passed on to all humans through procreation. Saint Paul tells us that "sin came into the world through one man and death through sin" (Rom. 5:12). Adam and Eve lost the supernatural grace they received at creation, so all human beings born after them come into the world without it, stained by our first parents' "original sin." In a mysterious way, all human beings are in Adam "as one body of one man."[1] We are all included in his rebellion, just as we are all included in Christ's victory over sin. "Original sin" predisposes us to actual sin. This is why the Church baptizes infants. All the descendants of Adam and Eve are sinners in need of God's grace (see *Catechism*, nos. 403–4).

*[**Note:** Because every one of us is affected by the radical change that took place in Adam and Eve (see* Catechism, *nos. 403–4), their response to God and to each other in the next few verses will be of particular interest to us.]*

2. Adam and Eve might well have expected God to mete out punishment then and there. But instead, He asked a number of questions: "Where are you? Who told you that you were naked? What is this thing that you have done?" Surely God knew all this already.

    a. Why do you think He asked these questions?

_____

_____

_____

_____

    b. *Challenge question:* Why is this interrogation by God actually a sign of *hope* for Adam and Eve?

_____

_____

_____

_____

3. God asked the man if he had disobeyed.

    a. How did Adam's response to God (v. 12) show the effect of the change in him caused by eating the forbidden fruit?

_____

_____

_____

_____

    b. How was the woman's response similar (v. 13)?

_____

_____

_____

---

[1] Saint Thomas Aquinas, *De Malo*, 4, 1

4. In these exchanges between God and His creatures, there was a glaring omission on the part of Adam and Eve. What was it?

_____

_____

_____

_____

5. *Challenge question:* God had told Adam and Eve that they would die if they ate the fruit. They did not drop dead upon eating the fruit, as if they'd bitten into poison. (The serpent had told a partial truth when he told them they wouldn't die as a result of eating.)
   a. From this passage, make a list of all the consequences of man's disobedience in the Garden. What kind of death had God meant?

_____

_____

_____

_____

   b. Do you think Adam and Eve knew they were experiencing this death?

_____

_____

_____

Curse and Promise
⚮ Read Gen. 3:14–15
*[**Note:** Before we proceed, let us pause long enough to make sure we read between the lines. In the face of Adam and Eve's complete blindness to their living death, as is evidenced by their lack of remorse, what might God have been justified in doing? We would find no fault in Him if He declared, "You ungrateful wretches—away with the likes of you!" He didn't do that. This is a moment in which we can dare to let hope grow. Does He still love them? Watch for the clues.]*

6. Having listened to their excuses, God pronounced a judgment. Why do you suppose He began His response to Adam and Eve's disobedience by cursing the *serpent* (vv. 14–15)?

_____

_____

_____

_____

7. Remember that when God spoke to the serpent, He was actually addressing the devil. What would the devil's destiny be, according to the imagery of verse 14? (Read also Is. 14:12–15; Lk. 10:17–19; Rev. 12:7–9; 20:7–10).

_____

_____

_____

_____

8. In verse 15, God announced a battle (that's what "enmity" means).
a. Did a battle already exist in the universe?

_____

_____

_____

_____

b. How did God's announcement change it?

_____

_____

_____

_____

9. Why do you suppose the battle would begin between the serpent and "the woman"?

_____

_____

_____

_____

The "First Gospel"

"After his fall, man was not abandoned by God. On the contrary, God calls him and in a marvelous way heralds the coming victory over evil and his restoration from his fall [cf. Gen. 3:9, 15]. This passage in Genesis is called the *Protoevangelium* ('first gospel'): the first announcement of the Messiah and Redeemer, of a battle between the serpent and the Woman, and of the final victory of a descendant of hers." (*Catechism*, no. 410)

---

*[**Note:** As we think carefully about "the woman" and "her seed" in Genesis, it is almost impossible not to think also of the fulfillment of this promise in Jesus and Mary. For the sake of our study, however, we will delay until lessons six and seven our examination of how Jesus and Mary were the New Adam and the New Eve. For now, we will work only with the Genesis passage.]*

10. We need to determine everything we can about this "woman" and "her seed."
a. First, if they will both engage in battle against God's enemy, how will they be *different* from Adam and Eve?

_____

_____

_____

_____

33

b. In Hebrew thought, men have "seed," not women. The phrase "her seed" is highly irregular. What question does it lead you to ask?

_____

_____

_____

_____

11. The "seed" of the "woman" will bruise the head of the serpent, while the serpent will bruise his heel.

a. What is the difference between these two kinds of wounds?

_____

_____

_____

_____

b. What does the difference in the wounds help us to understand about the outcome of this battle?

_____

_____

_____

_____

c. What will make this battle a particularly stunning humiliation for the devil?

_____

_____

_____

_____

d. Why will this battle be a breathtaking sign of hope for the humans?

_____

_____

_____

_____

❧

"Did Not Our Hearts Burn Within Us?"

Our hearts will burn with joy when we consciously open them wide to God's Word. Scripture memorization is a good way to get that started. Here is a suggested memory verse:

> _I will put enmity between you and the woman, and between your seed and her seed; he shall bruise your head, and you shall bruise his heel._
>
> —_Gen. 3:15_

Continue to welcome Him into your soul by reflecting on these questions:

To stand naked and exposed before God can cause us such pain that, like Adam and Eve, we try to find ways to cover it. We make excuses, we stay too busy, we spend our energy on the faults of others. Ask God for the grace to be honest about those places in your life that you try to cover with fig leaves. He can't heal you if you won't show Him the wound.

_____
_____
_____
_____

Although God knew exactly what had happened in the Garden, He asked for a verbal accounting of what Adam and Eve had done. Here we see, in its original context, what God wants men to do when they disobey Him: we must confess it. In addition to exposing ourselves to Him, we must take responsibility for our actions in a very human way—with words. Are you taking advantage of the opportunity to do this in the Sacrament of Reconciliation? This is how the Church preserves that moment in the Garden, enabling us to confess our sin, to detest it, to resolve not to repeat it, and to receive forgiveness. Consider how to make this a regular practice in your life.

_____
_____
_____
_____

Did it break your heart to watch Adam and Eve not recognize God's love for them? Ask Him to help you recognize His love for you even when it comes in a form that frightens you.

_____
_____
_____
_____

Take a few moments to *make sure* you fully comprehend God's love for you as manifested in this lesson. If Adam and Eve, in their rebellion, did not stop God's love, what can that mean for His love for you? You might want to be on your knees when you think about this.

_____
_____
_____
_____

❦

"Stay with Us"

What kind of eyesight is it that leads to blindness? It is the false sight that Adam and Eve received as the promise from the serpent. Their vision was so distorted and disordered that they could no longer see God, each other, or even themselves properly. The consequences of their choice to disobey God were seen immediately in this part of Genesis. Working hard to make themselves presentable and cover their shame, they made clear that all of us, whether we want to admit it or not, know deep inside of ourselves that something is *wrong* with us. Blinded in our inherited human nature, we sometimes try to cover this feeling of shame with bravado, accomplishments, or activity. Sometimes we numb our awareness of it through sensual inebriation. We fall victim to endless "self-esteem" concerns, always trying to overcome the drag we feel on our souls. We are like Lady Macbeth, washing and washing but not coming clean: "Out, out, damned spot!" And that is only the beginning.

As God approached His rebellious children in the Garden, in an attempt to draw them to Himself and examine what had gone wrong, they fled and hid. They perceived His nearness as trouble instead of as help. Given every opportunity to renounce what they had done and throw themselves on His mercy, they perceived His questions as accusations instead of as fatherly concern. Not recognizing that acknowledging their fault was the first step towards its remedy, they cast the blame away from themselves, making rehabilitation impossible. Man not only had a death sentence hanging over his head, but he was also walled in by spiritual blindness. How would God ever penetrate man's world?

As we examined this part of Genesis, one thing became perfectly clear: if there was to be a solution, it must come *entirely* at God's initiative. Adam and Eve were in no position to help themselves. They were barely able to even perceive the magnitude of the problem, let alone remedy it. If God truly loved these creatures and did not intend to give up on them, He would have to do all the work to save them from disaster.

That's precisely what He did. The first step He took to undo the catastrophe set the tone for the rest of man's history. God promised to defeat His enemy, the devil, through an astounding reversal. Human beings—"the woman and her seed"—would engage in a divine battle and prevail. In one glittering promise, God declared His authority over the devil, His love for humanity, and His chosen method of operation—reversal. If this is the way it *really* is between God and man, what is there to fear? As Saint Paul exuberantly asks, "If God is for us, who is against us?" (Rom. 8:31).

Lesson Summary

✔ The knowledge of good and evil that Adam and Eve received from the forbidden fruit was the knowledge of experience. Where once there was only goodness, now there was shame, danger, and blame. In the twinkling of an eye, although nothing in their environment had changed, everything inside of them did. They lost the grace God gave them at creation to see truthfully and live accordingly. They lost "original justice"—perfect love of God and man—with their "original sin."

✔ Although God would have been justified in eliminating these creatures and perhaps starting over, He sought them out, even as they hid from Him, and tried to draw out from them an accounting of what they had done. Instead of accepting this as help, they rejected it as an intrusion, trying to preserve innocence that had already been lost.

✔ It appeared that God had a plan to continue with mankind, but first He dealt with His enemy and theirs—the serpent. He condemned the devil to a life as the least of all creatures (and this was the one who had chided Adam and Eve for their creaturely submission). Beyond that, He declared that one day, human beings—a "woman" and "her seed"—would finish the battle begun that day. The "seed" would be the one to strike the deciding blow to the devil, although he would be bruised in the process. A woman and her son would restore the dignity of male and female lost in the Garden.

✔ The pair to come would be not in the devil's grip. They would be in opposition to, not in collusion with, the enemy. These two provoke our curiosity; they are humans worth waiting for.

For responses to Lesson 4 Questions, see pp. 115–19.

Paradise Lost
(Genesis 3:16–24)

Being present at the spiritual autopsy of Adam and Eve, as we were in our last lesson, was sobering. The death through disobedience that God warned them to avoid was immediate and complete. Their bodies didn't die, but something inside them did. They were still spiritual and corporeal beings—they retained their souls—but their ability to see spiritual realities correctly was lost. They did not become like the animals, without self-consciousness. They knew God existed. But their vision of Him was distorted, as was their vision of each other and themselves. The Church teaches us that what died in Adam and Eve was the supernatural life of *grace*. God created them with natural and spiritual faculties (body and soul). By His grace in them, their spiritual faculties were meant to keep their bodies' natural faculties under control. Just as there had been order in the universe, there was order within human nature. That harmony in man's nature died in the Garden. Adam and Eve broke the covenant God had made with them and with all creation. Stepping out of the covenant, they stepped into chaos.

We saw the signs of that chaos as soon as God approached them. But we also saw signs of something else. The outline of hope slowly began to take shape in the midst of the rubble. There was nothing in the humans to give rise to it, but the promise of God to defeat His enemy through the "woman" and "her seed" permeated the darkness with a shaft of light. Just as the chaos that once existed on the earth, when it was "without form" (Gen. 1:2), had been dispelled by God speaking ("And God said . . ."), a Word of promise from Him was the first step in rescuing man from the chaos of sin.

At this point in the story, the focus is not so much on Adam and Eve. We would much rather keep our eyes on God, who showed Himself to be entirely in control of everything and everyone, including the devil. He had a battle plan in place. He was not about to give up on His children. He appeared as Love itself. The goodness that infused creation in the first two chapters of Genesis was not just cosmetic. Truly, it was an overflow from the One we observe here—the presence of Love in the ruins.

But what will happen next? We can be cheered by the hope of the continuation of mankind, and we are certainly very curious about "the woman" and "her seed," with whom mankind's future seems so intimately linked. We are confident that God actually *loved* these creatures, even though they themselves struggled to perceive it. Will everyone and everything carry on as usual until the unusual duo of Mother and Son appear? Was spiritual death the end of God's punishment of Adam and Eve? To answer these questions, we must press on to finish Genesis 3.

🎜

"He Opened to Us the Scriptures"

Before we read God's Word, we ought to take a moment to humble ourselves before Him, remembering that His Word is primarily a conversation with us, not a textbook. "Speak, Lord, for thy servant hears" (1 Sam. 3:10) can be the prayer on our lips. Then, read all the way through Genesis 3:16–24, included in the lesson. Think about what you understand and what you don't understand. Make a simple response to God in terms of what you do understand. Write your prayer in this space:

_____

_____

_____

_____

_____

Now, ask for His help as you work on the questions below.
(Prayer hint: *"Lord, help me to remember that disobedience
to Your Word will bring me misery, not happiness."*)

🎜

Questions
Disobedience Punished

🎜 **Read Gen. 3:16–19**

1. Before we examine this passage, there are some questions we need to consider. All of us are children of parents; some of us are parents of children. Because of that, we are equipped to answer these:

a. Why do good parents punish their children?

_____

_____

_____

_____

b. *Challenge question:* Why is punishment always a sign of *hope*? Read Hebrews 12:4–11 before answering.

_____

_____

_____

_____

2. Look at God's punishment on Eve (v. 16). This is the first appearance of physical pain in the story of man. Describe how Eve was to experience punishment for disobedience in her life.

_____

_____

_____

_____

3. Look at God's punishment on Adam (vv. 17–19). We know already that marriage was to feel the effect of God's punishment, which Adam would have experienced.

a. Why do you think Adam's "rule" over his wife would cause him anguish, too?

_____

_____

_____

_____

b. *Challenge question:* To appreciate God's original intention for marriage, it is helpful to read what Saint Paul wrote about it in his epistle to the Ephesians. There, he helped Christians understand the sacred character of the marital bond. Read Ephesians 5:21–32. Although a husband is "the head of his wife," (v. 23), how is a Christian husband's authority different from the domination or "rule" of Genesis 3:16?

_____

_____

_____

_____

c. Beyond suffering in marriage, describe the unique punishment God gave to Adam for his disobedience.

_____

_____

_____

_____

Marriage: Sacrament of Christ and His Church

Spouses not only image the love of God within the Trinity; they also image the love between God and all humanity, made visible in the love of Christ and the Church. By virtue of their baptisms, the marriage of Christians is a sacrament. That means it's a living sign that truly communicates and participates in the union of Christ and the Church. The marriage vows lived out in the spouses' "one flesh" union constitute this living sign.

Paraphrasing Saint Paul: For this reason a man will leave father and mother and cling to his bride, and the two shall become one flesh. This is a profound mystery, *and it refers to Christ and the Church* (see Eph. 5:31–32). Christ left His Father in heaven. He left the home of His mother on earth—to give up His body for His Bride, so that we might become "one flesh" with Him.

Where do we become "one flesh" with Christ? Most specifically in the Eucharist. The Eucharist is the sacramental consummation of the marriage between Christ and the Church. And when we receive the body of our heavenly Bridegroom into our own, just like a bride we conceive new life in us—God's very own life. As Christ said, "Unless you eat the flesh of the Son of man and drink his blood, you have no life in you" (Jn. 6:53).

Since the "one flesh" communion of man and wife foreshadowed the Eucharistic communion of Christ and the Church right from the beginning, John Paul II speaks of marriage as the "primordial sacrament." Let's pause a moment to let this reality sink in. Of all the ways that God chooses to reveal his life and love in the created world, John Paul II is saying, that marriage—enacted and consummated by sexual union—is the most fundamental.

Saint Paul wasn't kidding when he said this is a "profound mystery." Could God have made our sexuality any more important than this? Any more beautiful? Any more glorious? God gave us sexual desire itself to be the power to love as he loves, so that we could participate in divine life and fulfill the very meaning of our being and existence.[1]

4. *Challenge question:* As we saw clearly in Genesis 3:7–15, Adam and Eve died spiritually because of their disobedience, with the terrible consequence of spiritual blindness. That seemed like a severe punishment. Yet as we can see from these verses, God punished each of them in additional ways. Why do you think He added these punishments?

_____

_____

_____

_____

---

[1] Reprinted from West, *Good News*, 20–21.

5. Look at the sentence pronounced on man and woman at the end of verse 19. Read Genesis 2:7. What was tragically clear about the consequence of sin in this final punishment from God?

_____
_____
_____
_____

A Severe Mercy

🔥 **Read Gen. 3:20–24**

6. God finished pronouncing His punishment on the humans. They made a start at resuming their lives. The first thing Adam did was name his wife. This prompts several questions:

a. What did this naming episode suggest about Adam's relationship to Eve?

_____
_____
_____
_____

b. Adam named his wife "Eve," which meant "Mother of all living." What do you think is the meaning of a name like that?

_____
_____
_____
_____

7. See that God clothed the humans with animal skins instead of the fig leaves they had sewed. What did this act reveal about God?

_____
_____
_____
_____

8. *Challenge question:* For skins to be made into garments, an innocent animal had to die in the Garden. What does this fact add to our understanding of the shame caused by man's disobedience and God's provision for it?

_____
_____
_____
_____

9. In verse 22, God had another "us" conversation, indicating that He was not alone.
a. Why was He concerned about Adam and Eve eating from the Tree of Life?

_____

_____

_____

_____

b. God sent Adam and Eve out of the Garden rather than simply getting rid of the tree. Why do you think He allowed the tree to continue to exist on the earth, under heavy guard?

_____

_____

_____

_____

10. *Challenge question:* Think about Adam and Eve as they were expelled from the Garden. Look back over Genesis 3 and write down every evidence you can find that God still loved and cared for His human creatures.

_____

_____

_____

_____

"Did Not Our Hearts Burn Within Us?"

Our hearts will burn with joy when we consciously open them wide to God's Word. Scripture memorization is a good way to get that started. Here is a suggested memory verse:

You are dust, and to dust you shall return.

—Gen. 3:19

Continue to welcome Him into your soul by reflecting on these questions:

One thing that has become crystal clear in our study of Genesis is that suffering does *not* mean that God doesn't love us. The story of Adam and Eve helps us to plant our feet firmly on the solid ground of God's unconquerable love. This unseen reality is the one that gives the seen realities their meaning. Is there suffering in your life now? Are you allowing it to have its full meaning? Reflect on anything you've learned in this lesson that might have the power to transform your experiences of suffering.

_____

_____

_____

Read Psalm 51 prayerfully as an offering to God for the tragedy of human sin.

Take some time to review, with specific details, why God has proved Himself to be *trustworthy* in this part of Genesis. No one who studies the first three chapters of this book should leave them without taking a moment to contemplate why it is that men should be able to trust God. Do you trust Him with your life?

_____

_____

_____

_____

❧ "Stay with Us"

Think of how far we've traveled in our study of the first three chapters of Genesis. Remember the glory of hearing God say, "Let us make man in our image, after our likeness" in Genesis 1:26? And now we hear, "[Y]ou are dust, and to dust you shall return" (3:19). We watched in silence as God drove man out of the Garden. We knew that God was not finished with the humans. But, at this point, we have more questions than answers.

We recognized that in the punishments God gave to Adam and Eve, He allowed them to suffer. This He did as any good father does. It was a temporary harshness aimed at rehabilitation. The woman would face pain and suffering in marriage and childbirth. These were places in her life where she should experience her greatest joy, for it was in these that she would fulfill her divine vocation. The suffering was meant to remind her that something had gone dreadfully wrong in human existence. It would present her with many occasions to cry out to God for help, returning her to her proper place in creation as a child dependent on her father. Adam likewise would sweat and toil to do the job God had given him. Subduing the earth would be a fight. And off in the distance was the inevitability of death. There would be no time for the charade of autonomy and defiance.

Yet even in the sad details of defeat and loss, God took charge. He allowed the man to name his wife, showing that even though they have fallen into spiritual chaos, He was willing to let them continue, as best they could, the life He had ordained for them. He did not want His creatures to be naked and defenseless. He clothed them with durable garments, which they would surely need as they were forced to leave the sanctuary of the Garden. The Tree of Life remained, but these creatures were prevented from returning to eat its healing leaves.

The humans left the Garden not just with new clothes but also with *hope*. They waited for a "woman" and "her seed" to appear so that their mortal enemy could be silenced. And they might well have wondered whether they or their descendants would someday be allowed to return to the Garden. Only God knew.

As we complete this part of our study of Genesis, we are ready to make the New Testament connections that have been begging to be made. We have made every effort to examine the story of our first parents as if we didn't know what happened next. This kind of approach always takes an effort, but it is the only one that enables us to stay focused on the action at hand. Now, however, we want to follow up on God's announcement that the hope of the whole word was pinned on "the woman" and "her seed." Who are they? When will they appear on the horizon of human history? Our next two lessons will be devoted entirely to them.

Lesson Summary

✔ God punished Eve and Adam in ways distinctive to their vocations. Pain and misery would characterize the most important parts of their lives. Even the earth suffered from their disobedience. In addition, they faced the dissolution of their physical bodies in death.

✔ Because we know that God loved these creatures and hadn't given up on them, this punishment can have only one meaning: it would serve to make it impossible for them, in their lives on earth, to realize the happiness they were designed to have. They would be restless, feeling their weakness and vulnerability, and always longing for *something more*. Perhaps they would cry out to God for help.

✔ Man and woman resumed the life God had ordained for them, although it underwent a radical difference. Adam named his wife Eve "Mother of all living," a name which represented the hope that through her motherhood, mankind had a future.

✔ God clothed His children with animal skins. He cared for them and did not abandon them. This covering of their nakedness required the death of an innocent animal, a drastic measure. It signified what God was willing to do to protect them in their shame.

✔ Adam and Eve were expelled from the Garden lest they live forever by eating from the Tree of Life. The Garden was placed under angelic guard. Perhaps as they left, they longed for the day when an angel would announce the good tidings of great joy—that Paradise could be regained.

For responses to Lesson 5 Questions, see pp. 119–23.

Mary, the "Woman"
(Genesis 3:5)

Before we proceed with our study of Genesis, in this lesson and the next we will take a departure from the Old Testament into the New. We are eager now to examine how God's promise to defeat His enemy through human beings, made so long ago, was finally fulfilled. Because the details of life in the Garden, presided over by Adam and Eve, are so vivid for us, we are perfectly prepared to recognize Mary and Jesus as the Woman and her Seed. This is an especially valuable step for Catholic students of Scripture. We have sometimes been misunderstood by our Protestant brethren to have imposed Mary upon the plan of Redemption in an unbiblical way. But as this lesson will show, Catholics simply continue today what Christians from the earliest centuries did when, having studied Genesis as we have done, they recognized that the Woman of Genesis 3:15 has always been part of God's plan to win the world back to Himself.

Our format in these lessons, because they are topical studies, will be different from usual. Instead of studying only one text, we will be reading various New Testament passages in order to make the necessary connections from Adam and Eve to Jesus and Mary. The purpose of these lessons is to enable you to hold together in your mind and heart various scenes from Scripture—the Garden of Eden, the Annunciation, the Garden of Gethsemane, and others. This will not be so much a time in which you dig out information as it will be a time for you to "see" the marvelous plan of God unfold, in exquisite beauty and power. The Church has always recognized meanings in Scripture beyond the literal. These lessons will enable us to explore the spiritual sense of the story of the Garden that we have so carefully examined (*Catechism*, no. 115).

First, however, we will need some idea of what happened between the Garden of Eden and the Annunciation. Some of this history will unfold as we proceed in our study of Genesis. Without giving away too much of the story, we need to know that from among all the descendants of Adam and Eve who multiplied and covered the earth, God formed for Himself one, unique nation, Israel, and entered into a covenant with it for a unique purpose. He made a promise to the father of this nation, Abraham, that through him and his descendants, God would return to all mankind the blessing lost in the Garden of Eden (Gen. 12:1–3). In some ways, the history of Israel paralleled the history of man in the Garden. The Israelites began as a people with blessings and gifts from God, just as Adam and Eve had. God wanted them to use their national life in priestly service to bring all the nations of the earth back to Himself. But they frequently rebelled against Him, violating the terms of the covenant He had made with them. Eventually, they suffered God's punishment and exile from their homeland. They became a subjugated people. Even when they were allowed to return to their own country, they were under the yoke of oppression by various nations that were stronger (and sometimes much more evil) than they were. Just as in the Garden, a time of glory was followed by a time of humiliation and loss.

All was never completely lost, however. In spite of rebellion and failure, God promised Israel, through prophets He sent to them, that someone was coming to restore them to greatness. Thus began the longing in Israel for the "Messiah" or "anointed one" to appear, the one who would defeat their enemies and set them free. We can't help but be struck by how this messianic expectation fits exactly the prophecy of Genesis 3:15.

It is almost as if an icon of a "woman" and her "seed" sits above all the troubled picture that was the history of Israel. Indeed, the Prophet Isaiah announced to King Ahaz that God wanted to give His people a sign of hope in the midst of their darkness. What would that sign be? As Isaiah 7:14 says, "Therefore the Lord Himself will give you a sign: Behold, the virgin shall conceive and bear a son and shall call his name Immanuel" (NAB).

By the year 4 BC (the presumed date of Jesus' birth), the air in Jerusalem was thick with anticipation of the appearance of the Messiah. If only he would come, the darkness of oppression by the enemy would be shattered. When would it happen?

𝕤

"He Opened to Us the Scriptures"

Before we read God's Word, we ought to take a moment to humble ourselves before Him, remembering that His Word is primarily a conversation with us, not a textbook. "Speak, Lord, for thy servant hears" (1 Sam. 3:10) can be the prayer on our lips. Because there are several Scripture passages to examine in this lesson, we suggest that you read the Magnificat of Mary (Lk. 1:46–55) as a prayer of praise to God as you begin this study.

_____

_____

_____

_____

_____

Now, ask for His help as you work on the questions below.

⸙
Questions
The Annunciation
⸙ **Read Lk. 1:26–38**

1. Look at the greeting of the angel to Mary in 1:28. In the Revised Standard Version–Catholic Edition, it is rendered, "Hail, full of grace!" Remember that the first notable characteristic of "the woman" of Genesis 3:15 was that she would be outside of the devil's influence. She, together with her "seed," would be co-laborers with God against His enemy. Why does this angelic greeting suggest that Mary stood in that unique place?

_____

_____

_____

_____

2. In Genesis 3:15, we puzzled over why there was no mention of a husband/father in the promise of the woman and her seed.

    a. What did the message from the angel reveal as the solution to that puzzle?

_____

_____

_____

_____

    b. For a woman to be "overshadowed" by the Holy Spirit and thus conceive the Son of God made her a most extraordinary woman. What effect might this news have had on her betrothed husband, Joseph? (Read also Mt. 1:18–25.)

_____

_____

_____

_____

3. Both Eve and Mary had conversations with angels.

    a. At the bidding of a fallen angel, Eve took action. What was it? (See Gen. 3:6.)

_____

_____

_____

_____

    b. In the Gospel, at the bidding of the angel, Gabriel, Mary also took action. What was it? (Lk. 1:38)

_____

_____

_____

_____

c. *Challenge question:* How was Mary's action at the Annunciation a reversal of what Eve did in the Garden?

_____

_____

_____

_____

The New Adam and the New Eve

The key to understanding why Catholics and Protestants differ so much on Mary is that each group has a different starting point. Protestants begin in the New Testament and, based on the relatively few passages about her there, conclude that Mary is a relatively minor player in the saga of Redemption. Catholics, however, begin in Genesis; so we arrive at the New Testament passages about Mary with vastly different expectations of her. Why do Catholics begin in Genesis to understand Mary? Let us look to Saint Paul for answers.

In some of the most important New Testament passages about the Person of Jesus and the nature of His work for us, Saint Paul refers to Jesus as "the last Adam" (1 Cor. 15:42–49; Rom. 5:12–14). Why did Saint Paul go all the way back to the Garden of Eden to help Christians better understand Jesus? The answer lies in the angel's declaration to Mary, recorded in Luke's Gospel. Jesus would be conceived by the Holy Spirit (Lk. 1:35); He would be the Son of God, as well as Mary's son. Saint Paul knew that the first "son of God" had been Adam, who had been brought to life from dust by the "breath" or "spirit" of God. The parallels Paul drew between Adam and Jesus formed a helpful framework for Christians to understand the magnitude of Christ's work on earth and His role in God's eternal plan, evident even in Genesis, to restore fallen mankind to Paradise.

It was only a matter of time (and not very much) before Christians who read Genesis to understand Jesus also recognized Mary as the "New Eve." To see Mary as the New Eve was a very natural development in early Christianity. In fact, we have evidence of it in the writings of the very first great Christian apologist, Saint Justin Martyr (c. AD 110–165). In his defense of the faith, *Dialogue with Trypho,* he writes:

[The Son of God] became man through a Virgin, so that the disobedience caused by the serpent might be destroyed in the same way it had begun. For Eve, who was virgin and undefiled, gave birth to disobedience and death after listening to the serpent's words. But the Virgin Mary conceived faith and joy; for when the angel Gabriel brought her the glad tidings that the Holy Spirit would come upon her and that the power of the Most High would overshadow her, so that the Holy One born of her would be the Son of God, she answered, "Let it be done to me according to your word" (Lk. 1:38). Thus was born of her the [Child] about whom so many Scriptures speak, as we have shown.

Through him, God crushed the serpent, along with those angels and men who had become like serpents.[1]

It is important to understand that Saint Justin Martyr was writing a defense of the Christian faith against attacks from the Jews and pagans. He was not developing new theological insight. He was only defending what the Church believed and taught at that early time in her history. The development of Marian theology was as early as the development of the doctrine of the Trinity. It took Christians hundreds of years to formulate explicitly the doctrine of the Trinity, a word that doesn't appear in Scripture. Time is not the enemy of truth. The question is not whether a doctrine took time to develop but whether the seed of that doctrine was contained in the Gospel preached and taught by the apostles. That is what this lesson on Mary aims to discover.

The Visitation

🎵 **Read Lk. 1:39–56**

4. As mentioned in the introduction to this lesson, we can think of the promise of "the woman" and "her seed" in Genesis 3:15 as a kind of icon of Mother and Child that was printed over all the history of Israel. Their appearance, whenever it happened, would herald the defeat of God's enemy, which would be a source of great joy among the Jews. Look carefully at Luke 1: 39–45. Elizabeth and the son in her womb were the very first Jews to recognize the appearance of the Mother and Child.

a. How does this scene fulfill our expectation of how the people of Israel should react when the Mother and Child appeared?

_____

_____

_____

_____

b. *Challenge question:* How do these verses help us to understand that the joy of Elizabeth and John was caused by *both* Mary and Jesus?

_____

_____

_____

_____

5. From what we have seen of Mary thus far, she was a meek and humble girl. Look at what she said in verse 48. Mary prophesied that all generations to come after her would call her "blessed." Indeed, to this day we know her as the "Blessed Virgin Mary."

---

[1] As quoted in Luigi Gambero, *Mary and the Fathers of the Church: The Blessed Virgin Mary in Patristic Thought*, trans. Thomas Buffer (San Francisco: Ignatius Press, 1999), 47.

a. Read the *Catechism*, nos. 148–49. Why do we call Mary "blessed"?

_____

_____

_____

_____

b. *Challenge question:* Read Luke 11:27–28. Sometimes non-Catholics who believe the Church exaggerates the importance of Mary refer to these verses to show that even in Jesus' own day, people tried to make too much of His mother. It seems to them that Jesus did not want anyone to honor His mother; rather, honor is for those "who hear the word of God and do it." As a Catholic, how would you interpret these verses?

_____

_____

_____

_____

The Presentation in the Temple

 **Read Lk. 2:22–35**

[Note: In this Gospel scene, we see Joseph and Mary presenting Jesus to God at the Temple in Jerusalem. Simeon is described as a devout man "waiting for the consolation of Israel," which means he, like many others, was looking for the Messiah. Inspired by the Holy Spirit, he blessed them and prophesied over them.]

6. Look at verses 33–35. Earlier, in the Visitation, Elizabeth, who had been filled with the Holy Spirit, announced that Jesus *and* Mary shared in the blessing of God: "Blessed are you among women, and blessed is the fruit of your womb." What else would Jesus and Mary share, according to Simeon's prophecy? (Read also *Catechism*, no. 964, 618.)

_____

_____

_____

_____

The Wedding at Cana

 **Read Jn. 2:1–11**

[Note: If we read the very first words of John's Gospel, we know that he wanted to evoke for his readers the creation account in Genesis. "In the beginning was the Word" (1:1) sets the stage for the first few chapters of his Gospel. John wanted his readers to understand that the coming of Jesus into the world was going to initiate a restoration of God's original intentions for His creation. At the wedding in Cana, Jesus addressed His mother as "woman," very reminiscent of "the woman" of Genesis 3:15.]

7. We know that Jesus and Mary shared God's blessing (Lk. 1:42) and they would share suffering (Lk. 2:35). At Cana, how did Mary also share in the work Jesus came to do? (See also *Catechism,* no. 2618.)

_____

_____

_____

_____

The Crucifixion

Read Jn. 19:25–27

8. *Challenge question:* We know that Adam named his wife, "Mother of all living," (Gen. 3:20), a name full of hope. In John's Gospel, Jesus gave His mother to John, the only apostle at the foot of the Cross. She was to be his mother, too. Jesus again addressed her as "woman," evoking the early chapters of Genesis. How did the gift of Mary to John fulfill the hope expressed in Adam's name for his wife, "Eve"? (Read also *Catechism,* no. 726.)

_____

_____

_____

_____

A Vision of Heaven

Read Rev. 12:1–17

[**Note:** *This is a scene from a vision of heaven that the Apostle John had while he was on the island of Patmos. Remember the promise God made in Genesis 3:15 to put "enmity" between the woman and the serpent, between her seed and his.*]

9. Read verses 1–6.

a. Who are the woman and her child in verses 1–6?

_____

_____

_____

_____

b. The woman wears a crown of stars and is clothed with the sun and moon. What does this description of her clothing suggest to us about her status in heaven?

_____

_____

_____

_____

c. How did the dragon express his "enmity" against the woman and her son?

_____

_____

_____

_____

10. Read verses 7–17.
a. How was the dragon defeated (v. 11)?

_____

_____

_____

_____

b. Once the dragon had been cast out of heaven, against whom did he direct his wrath (vv. 13, 17)? (Read also *Catechism,* no. 2853.)

_____

_____

_____

_____

11. *Challenge question:* In Genesis, the Bible begins with a foreshadowing of Jesus and His Mother, Mary. Likewise, in Revelation, the Bible ends with a heavenly vision of Jesus and His Mother. Catholics have solid biblical reasons for keeping Mary as the icon of the "woman" and her "seed" from Genesis 3:15. However, many non-Catholic Christians live their lives with God without any reference or recourse to her. It is quite possible to live a fruitful Christian life without a true knowledge of Mary as the New Eve (as we see among our Protestant brethren). This must mean that the presence of Mary in the Catholic (and Orthodox) Church is a *gift* to the Church. A gift goes beyond what is "necessary." Look back over the passages in this lesson, pondering the person of Mary in each passage—her characteristics and her actions. What do they suggest is added to our lives as God's children when we receive Mary as a *gift* from Jesus?

_____

_____

_____

_____

❧

"Did Not Our Hearts Burn Within Us?"

Our hearts will burn with joy when we consciously open them wide to God's Word. Scripture memorization is a good way to get that started. Here is a suggested memory verse:

For behold, henceforth all generations will call me blessed; for he who is mighty has done great things for me, and holy is his name.

—*Lk. 1:48–49*

Continue to welcome Him into your soul by reflecting on these questions:

As Catholics, we are blessed with a great treasury of Christian art, which enables us frequently to visualizes some of the scenes we have studied in this lesson. One of the most precious of these scenes is the Annunciation. Do you have access to a picture or painting or some kind of representation of this scene? If so, put it before you and spend some time meditating on why it represents the most glorious moment in human history—and why it has made all the difference in your own personal history. Respond to God appropriately.

_____
_____
_____
_____

We have seen that when God acts, He makes use of reversals to accomplish His will. Where in your life now are you in need of reversal? Make every effort to put your trust in God to make darkness into light, to turn mourning into dancing. Be specific in your acts of faith. Be willing to be patient for God to act. He will not fail you.

_____
_____
_____
_____

The *Catechism* says: "What the Catholic faith believes about Mary is based on what it believes about Christ, and what it teaches about Mary illumines in turn its faith in Christ" (no. 487). What have you learned about Mary in this lesson that will strengthen and invigorate your life in Christ? She is the transparent window into life that is "full of grace." Look carefully at her, and ask her to be your advocate as you open your heart wide to all that God has to give you.

_____
_____
_____
_____

✹

"Stay with Us"

Now that we have pondered numerous New Testament scenes in which the Mother and Son are prominently featured, we know that the expectation that began to grow in Genesis 3 of two very remarkable human beings to arise in human history was not misdirected. If we pinned all our hopes on them when we left Paradise with Adam and Eve, we have not been disappointed. In this lesson, our focus has been on Mary as the New Eve. That impulse we felt to rewrite the story of the Fall of our first parents has been taken up by God Himself in the unfolding of the Gospel. His plan, in its beauty and perfection, far exceeds anything we could have imagined. We, quite probably, would not have given the humans such important roles in setting things right. We are still subject to the serpent's opinion of man and woman. Can the world be won back to God through mere mortals?

Perhaps the answer is best given by Saint Bernard of Clairvaux, as he pondered the Annunciation:

> We all have been made in the eternal Word of God, and look, we are dying. In your brief reply we shall be restored and so brought back to life. Doleful Adam and his unhappy offspring, exiled from Paradise, implore you, kind Virgin, to give this answer; David asks it, Abraham asks it; all the other holy patriarchs, your very own fathers beg it of you, as do those now dwelling in the region of the shadow of death. For it the whole world is waiting, bowed down at your feet. And rightly so, because on your answer depends the comfort of the afflicted, the redemption of captives, the deliverance of the damned; the salvation of all the sons of Adam, your whole race. Give your answer quickly, my Virgin. My lady, say this word which earth and hell and heaven itself are waiting for. . . . Are you the one who was promised, or must we look for another? No, it is you and no one else. You, I say, are the one we were promised, you are the one we are expecting.[2]

Lesson Summary

✔ The angel addressed Mary, a young virgin of Nazareth, with a greeting that marked her out as a human being unlike all others since the time of Adam and Eve—"full of grace." She was told that by the power of the Holy Spirit, she would bear a Son. He would be the Son of God and the Son of Mary. This Mother and Son must be "the woman" and her "seed" from Genesis 3:15.

---

[2] Homily 4, no. 8, in *Magnificat: Homilies in Praise of the Blessed Virgin,* trans. Marie-Bernard Said and Grace Perigo (Kalamazoo, MI: Cistercian Publications, 1979), 53–54.

✔ Mary's conversation with an angel and her humble obedience to God's Word were the opposite of Eve's disobedience. She submitted entirely to God's plan for His creation. Christians from the earliest history of the Church have seen in Mary a New Eve.

✔ When Mary visited her cousin, she and her Son in the womb were greeted with a blessing as well as an act of reverence by Elizabeth, who was filled with the Holy Spirit. Mary's voice also caused John the Baptist to rejoice in Elizabeth's womb. The darkness in which humanity had kept watch ever since the expulsion from the Garden was being penetrated by a great light, just as the darkness of Elizabeth's womb was brightened by the sound of Mary's voice.

✔ Mary shared the blessing of God with Jesus; she also shared His suffering. Simeon, filled with the Holy Spirit, spoke directly to her about this as she and Joseph presented Jesus to the Lord in the Temple. In a graphic prophecy, Simeon announced that Mary would suffer with her Son as He became the cause of the rise and fall of many in Israel. As Eve was Adam's helper to do the work God had given him to do, Mary joined her Son in the work God sent Him to accomplish.

✔ At Mary's request, Jesus performed the first of His miraculous signs that revealed Him to be Israel's Messiah at a wedding in Cana. Using language reminiscent of creation and the Garden of Eden, the Gospel writer helped us to recognize the New Adam and New Eve at work to transform lives of mere existence into lives with the richness of the finest wine.

✔ The name Adam gave to Eve, describing her as the "mother of all living," was given a spiritual fulfillment by Jesus while He was on the Cross. He gave Mary to John and John to Mary, establishing her as the Mother of His new family, the Church.

✔ In the Apocalypse of John, the woman and the child she bore were objects of the wrath of the devil. The child was caught up to heaven. By His blood, He defeated the dragon, who was thrown down to the earth. The woman was kept safe from the enemy by God's protection. In the short time he has left, the dragon makes war against the woman and her offspring, often understood as Mary and the Church.

For responses to Lesson 6 Questions, see pp. 123–27.

Jesus, the "Seed"
(Genesis 3:15)

In our lesson on Mary as "the woman" of Genesis 3:15, we observed something sur- prising begin to emerge. Studying the details of her life, we began to understand that the mother and son foretold in Genesis would not only appear someday to begin God's victorious battle against the devil, but they would, in a mysterious way, undo what went wrong in Adam and Eve. This is even more glorious than what we might have expected. It satisfies the longing all of us develop as we read the first three chapters of Genesis. Saint Paul is the one who alerts us to this grand plan, in his references to Adam as "a type of the one to come." The earliest Christians bear testimony in their writings that the Church continued to reflect on the relationship between "the woman" and her "seed" and a New Adam and New Eve. Already we have noted the comparison between Eve and Mary: Eve's conversation with a fallen angel led to the loss of God's likeness in human flesh; Mary's conversation with an angel led to the Incarnation, God taking on human flesh.

Eve, left exposed by her husband, talked herself out of being embarrassingly gullible in believing God's word about the forbidden fruit; Mary, full of grace through the work of her Son, chose God's will for her life, knowing the potential for embarrassment over her unusual pregnancy.

Eve, having broken the covenant she and Adam had with God, heard God's curse on her life, which would be pain in childbearing; Mary, having accepted God's plan, heard a voice of blessing on her and her childbearing.

Eve, Adam's helper, assisted him in entering the devil's bondage; Mary, at the wedding in Cana, assisted Jesus in showing Himself to be the Messiah who had come to free Israel.

Eve became the mother of the dying; Mary, the mother of the living. Eve was expelled from Paradise; Mary appeared as the Queen of Heaven.

Now we will continue our examination of the promise of Genesis 3:15. Having recognized "the woman" in Mary, we will also see the "seed" in Jesus, her Son. We will want to watch the details of Jesus' life to see why Saint Paul refers to Him as a second Adam. Was Adam's life, without the fall into sin, recapitulated in Jesus?

There's one more question we ought to ask ourselves. What does all this mean? If Jesus and Mary, in the details of the lives they lived, undid the wrong of Adam and Eve, what were the implications for humanity? Dare we let ourselves think that if we find within human history a New Adam and a New Eve, we might also find a new Garden of Eden, complete with beauty, goodness, and truth?

This lesson follows the format of the previous topical study.

※

"He Opened to Us the Scriptures"

Before we read God's Word, we ought to take a moment to humble ourselves before Him, remembering that His Word is primarily a conversation with us, not a textbook. "Speak, Lord, for thy servant hears" (1 Sam. 3:10) can be the prayer on our lips. In this lesson, because of the variety of texts, use the "Our Father," the prayer that Jesus gave His disciples, to prepare you to hear what God has to say to you.

_____

_____

_____

_____

_____

Now, ask for His help as you work on the questions below.

※

Questions
Jesus and the Devil

※ **Read Mt. 4:1–11**

※ **Read Lk. 22:39–46**

1. In an earlier lesson (lesson 3, question 6c.), we observed that the serpent in the Garden of Eden tempted the humans to cast off the mantle of creaturely dependence on God and to listen to the voice of pride and autonomy.

a. Read Matthew 4:1–11. Look carefully at how Satan tempted Jesus in the desert. How were those temptations similar to the one in the Garden?

_____

_____

_____

_____

b. How did Jesus counter them?

_____

_____

_____

_____

c. Read Luke 22:39–46. In this Gospel scene, which took place in another garden, Gethsemane, do you see any evidence of another kind of temptation?

_____

_____

_____

_____

2. See that Jesus' sweat fell to the ground "like great drops of blood" in this scene. Remember the Garden and God's punishment on Adam (see Gen. 3:19). What do you think is the significance of Jesus sweating in His own garden of temptation?

_____

_____

_____

3. Read Hebrews 5:7–10. This text reveals how Jesus met His temptation in Gethsemane. What difference might this kind of reaction have made for Adam in his garden?

_____

_____

_____

_____

Jesus, the New Adam

It wasn't just a coincidence that Jesus happened to be in a garden when He had to make His decision to choose God's will over His own, no matter what the cost. This was the moment when Jesus completed His work as the New Adam. The first Adam was silent and passive in the face of temptation. Jesus, well aware of what it would cost Him to obey God, put the will of the Father first. The pride of the first Adam was replaced by the humility of the Second Adam. If Adam shrank from the danger in his garden, giving into disobedience, Jesus rose to the challenge of the danger in His garden, surrendering Himself freely to God's plan. The undoing of the devil had begun. As the *Catechism* says, "The evangelists indicate the salvific meaning of this mysterious event: Jesus is the new Adam who remained faithful just where the first Adam had given in to temptation. . . . In this, Jesus is the devil's conqueror: he 'binds the strong man,' to take back his plunder [cf. Ps. 95:10; Mk. 3:27]. Jesus' victory over the tempter in the desert anticipates victory at the Passion, the supreme act of obedience of his filial love for the Father" (no. 539).

"Here Is the Man!"

🕊 **Read Jn. 19:1–11**

4. *Challenge question:* See that Pilate declared to those seeking to kill Jesus, "Here is the man!" (v. 5). How was that announcement by Pilate an unwitting fulfillment of Genesis 1:26?

_____
_____
_____
_____

5. Read verses 10–11. What was the source of the courage Jesus showed here which Adam lacked in the Garden?

_____
_____
_____
_____

A Return to Paradise

In Luke 23:43, Jesus promised one of the criminals next to him on the Cross: "Truly I say to you, today you will be with me in Paradise." As Tim Gray says in *Mission of the Messiah*:

> The word 'paradise' is only used two other times in the New Testament. Paul uses it to describe heaven (2 Cor. 12:3), and it is used in Revelation to describe heaven as the new Garden of Eden that Jesus promises to those who persevere in faithfulness: "To him who conquers I will grant to eat of the tree of life, which is in the paradise of God" (Rev. 2:7). Jesus completes on the Cross the return from the ultimate exile, the exile from the Father. With Jesus' last breath on the Cross, the exile from Eden ends, and heaven is reopened to Adam and his descendants.[1]

An Opened Side

🕊 **Read Jn. 19:31–37**

6. Look at verse 34. Recall that an opening in Adam's side produced his bride, Eve. Then read the *Catechism,* no. 1225. What was the significance of blood and water flowing from a wound in Christ's side?

_____
_____
_____
_____

---

[1] Tim Gray, *Mission of the Messiah* (Steubenville, OH: Emmaus Road, 1998), 144–45.

Jesus, the Gardener

𝄞 **Read Jn. 20:11–18**

7. *Challenge question:* We know that Jesus was buried in a garden (John 19:41). Thus, the Resurrection took place in a garden as well. Mary Magdalene mistook Jesus to be "the gardener" (20:15). What is the connection we can make between Jesus and Adam in this scene?

_____
_____
_____
_____

Suffering and Death

𝄞 **Read Heb. 2:5–18**

8. *Challenge question:* Look at verses 9–10 carefully. The writer says that "it was fitting" that God made Jesus "perfect" through suffering. This does not mean that Jesus was imperfect. "To perfect," in this context, means to advance to the final and complete fulfillment. Knowing what we know about life in (and out) of the Garden, why was it "fitting" for Jesus to suffer in order to reach His fulfillment as the "pioneer" of our salvation?

_____
_____
_____
_____

9. *Challenge question:* Look at verses 14–15. In Genesis 3:15, God said to the serpent, "he shall bruise your head and you shall bruise his heal." According to these verses, Jesus delivered that bruise through His own human death. His death destroyed the devil, who "has the power of death."

a. What do these verses suggest is the "power" the devil has in death?

_____
_____
_____
_____

b. Why would the death of Jesus have destroyed the devil's power?

_____
_____
_____
_____

*[**Note:** In this lesson and the previous one, we have recognized in New Testament texts all the clues that the "woman" and her "seed," Jesus and Mary, not only fulfilled the promise God made in the Garden of Eden, but did it in such a way that they recapitulated the first*

Adam and Eve. We are ready now to let ourselves think about a return to life in Paradise, where humans are blessed, not cursed, and where God's family thrives. In the Genesis story, we must wait until chapter 12 to see the outline of God's plan for blessing all mankind. However, it is worth considering now some New Testament evidence about how descendants of Adam and Eve can regain the life of Eden.]

A Surprising Solution

⚡ Read Jn. 3:1–15

10. In the Garden, we realized that Adam and Eve (and all their descendants) underwent a radical, systemic change in their human natures. In this conversation between Jesus and Nicodemus, what did Jesus present as the solution to this radical problem?

_____

_____

_____

_____

Eat and Live Forever

⚡ Read Jn. 6:47–59

11. Here is another occasion in which Jesus startled Jews with His teaching. Why was Jesus' offering of Himself as food and drink for immortality a sign that Eden could be regained?

_____

_____

_____

_____

The Church, the Goal of Eden

The signs are everywhere in the New Testament that the Woman and her Seed—Jesus and Mary—preside over new life in a regained Paradise, which is the Church. The Church is the family of God, people who are born anew through faith and baptism into the life of supernatural grace that was lost in Eden. It was always God's intention that men would have communion with His divine life. As Saint Clement of Alexandria tells us, "Just as God's will is creation and is called 'the world,' so his intention is the salvation of men, and it is called 'the Church.'"[2] The plan of God has never been thwarted. The *Catechism* assures us that even the fall of angels and men was only permitted by God in order for Him to demonstrate more magnificently His love for us and His power to save us (no. 760). Evil never has and never will triumph over Eden.

---

[2] *Paedagogus*, bk. 1, chap. 6, no. 27.

12. *Challenge question:* The Garden of Eden was both a spiritual and physical reality. The same is true today. The Church exists spiritually, among God's people, and it also exists in a physical way, when Christians gather together to give public demonstration of their faith in God and their desire to keep covenant with Him. They do this in churches.

Picture the inside of a traditional Catholic church. What are some of its features that evoke the Garden of Eden?

_____

_____

_____

_____

❧

"Did Not Our Hearts Burn Within Us?"

Our hearts will burn with joy when we consciously open them wide to God's Word. Scripture memorization is a good way to get that started. Here is a suggested memory verse:

> *Father, if thou are willing, remove this cup from me; nevertheless not my will, but thine, be done.*
>
> —Lk. 22:42

Continue to welcome Him into your soul by reflecting on these questions:

In the *Catechism*, we read an amazing statement: "Christ's whole life is a mystery of recapitulation. All Jesus did, said, and suffered had for its aim restoring fallen man to his original vocation" (no. 518). And also, "Christ enables us *to live in him* all that he himself lived, and *he lives it in us*" (no. 521). Think about your life as one who has been readmitted to the Garden of Eden. Is your love being tested? Do you hear a temptation to deny yourself nothing? What have you learned in this lesson about the power of Jesus' life that can see you through every struggle this day will bring?

_____

_____

_____

_____

_____

We understand from this lesson that Jesus defeated the devil by conquering death and the fear attached to it. If fear has a grip on you anywhere in your life, recognize it as a sham. Name that fear, and ask the New Adam to set you free.

🐝

"Stay with Us"

The Scriptures leave no doubt that all the stirrings of hope and anticipation we experienced in our study of the first chapters of Genesis, in spite of the tragedy of man's fall from grace, were not without foundation. As the Gospel story unfolds, we have seen all the clues that Mary and her Son, Jesus, are the long-promised "woman" and her "seed" from Genesis 3:15. By their faithful obedience, not only do they bring ruin to the devil, but they also become the human faces and bodies of a New Adam and New Eve. God's lost children, barred from the Tree of Life, have now received a way back into Eden. The Garden of the Church is a haven of safety in a hostile world. Although the children of the Church are still battered by an enemy, his time is short. In this Garden, the children enjoy the presence of the New Adam and New Eve and the community of love and holiness that was supposed to fill Eden. They eat freely of the Eucharist, the food that will give them eternal life. Theirs is a blessed, happy life.

The prayer that sustains these children in their life is the "Our Father." Think for a moment about this prayer. Knowing what we know about everything that happened in the first Eden, what kind of prayer do you think men and women would pray *if they were allowed back in?* What would they have learned from the experiences of Adam and Eve? With their restored spiritual sight, what would they say to God in their profound gratitude for being restored to what was lost, entirely through His goodness and grace?

Surely, they would adore and honor Him. *"Our Father, Who art in heaven, hallowed be Thy name."* They would recognize the need for obedience to His plan for creation, and that no other plan will do. *"Thy Kingdom come, Thy will be done, on earth as it is in heaven."* They would know that God provides the food they need. They would have no need to lust after forbidden fruit. *"Give us this day our daily bread."* They would be ready to confess their faults, which Adam and Eve tried to avoid. They would recognize the need to forgive others rather than laying blame. *"Forgive us our trespasses, as we forgive those who trespass against us."* They would live in dependence on God, knowing that an enemy stalks them. Their lives would be lived in humility and faith, not pride and autonomy. *"Lead us not into temptation, but deliver us from evil."*

The "Our Father" is the prayer of the New Eden. It says everything.

Lesson Summary

✔ The Gospel details of the life of Jesus lead to an inevitable comparison between Adam and Jesus. Not only was Jesus "the seed" of Genesis 3:15, who did battle with the devil, but He was also the Second Adam, undoing what went wrong in Eden:

- He chose to obey God in His garden of temptation, even though it meant terrible suffering and death.
- He cried out in faith to His Father instead of remaining silent in doubt, as Adam did.
- He began to take the curse of man's sin onto Himself, with sweat and thorns.
- A wound in His side while He was on the Cross became a symbol of His Bride, the Church, just as from a wound in Adam's side, God created Eve; the water of Baptism and blood of the Eucharist create a community of believers in union, body and soul, with Him.
- Jesus is the "gardener" of the New Eden; Mary, His Mother, is the first fruit of that Garden.

✔ In fulfillment of God's promise in Genesis, "the seed" defeated God's enemy, the devil, through a great reversal. Although His death on the Cross had the appearance of defeat, it was actually the beginning of victory. Because Jesus perfectly obeyed God, loving not His life to the end, God raised Him from the dead, breaking the bondage that comes through fear of death. The devil was left powerless in his battle with a human being ("he shall bruise your head"), just as God promised.

✔ The death and Resurrection of Jesus in a garden is meant to help us understand that He has made it possible for men to return to Eden. He took upon Himself the punishment of God on man's rebellion. The innocent suffered for the guilty. As a result, the guilty can be washed clean in the water of Baptism and receive the new life of a second birth through the Holy Spirit. They can once again live as God's blessed family.

✔ Jesus offered Himself as food for those who desire to live forever. In the Eucharist, men will enjoy "the medicine of immortality," just as they would have in Eden, eating from the Tree of Life.

✔ The Church, the New Eden, is the family of God, which is primarily a spiritual reality. But Catholic life in its physical expression, especially in churches, evokes many features of the original Garden. This preserves what God intended for man from the very beginning. It is a life that is *very good*.

For responses to Lesson 7 Questions, see pp. 127–32.

Life Outside of Eden
(Genesis 4–5)

It is time now to return to the story of Genesis. We have been fortified by our knowledge of what the New Testament reveals as the fulfillment of the promise of God in Genesis 3:15. We have allowed ourselves to peek ahead to see if the hope of a restoration and return to Eden, which we felt so strongly when Adam and Eve were expelled, could be possible. Now the challenge for us is to continue our study of Genesis as if we do not know what lies ahead. This will take some discipline, of course, but our study will be better for it.

We are now ready to see what happened to Adam and Eve once they left the sanctuary of Eden. Remember that when they left Paradise, even though they had lost their supernatural grace, and were consequently subject to sin, suffering, and death, they also left with concrete reasons for hope (read about these again, by way of review, in lesson 5, response 10). We ought to be full of questions about their new lives outside the Garden. What kind of relationship will the "dis-graced" humans have with God? What will they pass along to their offspring? What kind of civilization will develop from these people?

"He Opened to Us the Scriptures"

Before we read God's Word, we ought to take a moment to humble ourselves before Him, remembering that His Word is primarily a conversation with us, not a textbook. "Speak, Lord, for thy servant hears" (1 Sam. 3:10) can be the prayer on our lips. Then, read all the way through Genesis 4 and 5. Think about what you understand and what you don't understand. Make a simple response to God in terms of what you do understand. Write your prayer in this space:

_____

_____

_____

_____

_____

69

Now, ask for His help as you work on the questions below.
(Prayer hint: *"Lord, please grant that I will always accept
Your invitation to 'do well' rather than evil."*)

❧

Questions

*[**Note:** It is necessary for us to pick up the pace in the remainder of our study. Most of the rest of the lessons will cover at least two chapters of Genesis (Genesis is a big book!). Some of the chapters will be summarized in the lesson, without accompanying questions on the texts.]*

Firstfruits of the Fall

❧ **Read Gen. 4:1–7**

1. Look at Eve's comment after the birth of Cain (v. 1). She recognized that this son was a gift from God. Why was Eve's statement a hopeful sign in this new life outside Eden?

_____
_____
_____
_____

The Offerings of Cain and Abel

It is interesting to see that the sons of Adam and Eve both understood that offerings to God were necessary. Where would they have gotten that idea? Undoubtedly they had learned it from their parents. We can assume that Adam and Eve told their children everything that had happened to them in the Garden. They would have explained how they had disobeyed God and paid dearly for it. They would also have been able to testify to God's continued love and kindness for them, especially in the promise of defeat of God's enemy. The first knowledge that Cain and Abel had of God would have come to them through their parents.

The details about God and His creation that Adam and Eve passed on to their children would have been their offspring's first encounter with grace. Because of original sin, men, outside of Eden, would know that a Creator existed and that He was entitled to their reverence, but they would be dependent on additional information to know more than that. The story of Eden, with details of God's nature revealed in His actions both before and after the Fall of man, would have provided that extra knowledge. The creation story was a source of grace to Cain and Abel. It gave them what they couldn't have gotten for themselves. How did they respond to it?

Abel's response to the God of his parents was wholehearted and generous, which pleased the Lord (Heb. 11:4). He gave the best of the best; he must have believed that God was worthy of it. Cain, on the other hand, did not please the Lord, and his offering was not acceptable. It is important to see that "for Cain and his offering," God had "no regard" (Gen. 4:5). It was not simply that Cain had made the wrong offering. There was something in Cain himself that the Lord found displeasing. What could that have been? We don't know for sure, but perhaps Cain had made the offering perfunctorily, without generosity or gratitude. Perhaps he had offered the leftovers and not the "first" portion of his crop. God knew that Cain's offering reflected his heart. He knew that Cain was capable of something better, something more appropriate for creatures who are made in God's image. So, He rejected the lesser, in hopes for something better.

These two men give us the two responses possible to God's grace in the world. One response to the fact of God's existence is humble generosity of heart. The other response is proud resistance. Thus begins the story of life outside of Eden.

2. Cain was very angry over God's response to him and to his offering. What does this suggest to you about the kind of man Cain was?

_____

_____

_____

_____

3. God gave Cain the opportunity to worship Him in the right way, which opened wide the door to forgiveness and restoration (v. 7). It was a lavish offer of grace.
  a. If Cain refused God's offer and did not "do well," what problem did God tell him he would face?

_____

_____

_____

_____

  b. *Challenge question:* God's warning to Cain about not doing well (doing evil) suggests that sin has two consequences, not just one. Read Romans 6:16. What does Saint Paul say is the second consequence of sin (one that happens in addition to the first consequence, which is broken communion with God)? (Read also *Catechism,* no. 1472.)

_____

_____

_____

_____

4. Cain and Abel were born to the same parents and presumably had the same upbringing. What do you suppose explains the difference between them?

_____

_____

_____

_____

Cain Is Cursed

🔥 **Read Gen. 4:8–16**

5. See the details of Abel's murder in verse 8. What more do we understand from these details about the kind of man Cain was?

_____

_____

_____

_____

6. Surely God knew where Abel was; why do you think He asked Cain, "Where is Abel your brother?" (v. 9).

_____

_____

_____

_____

7. Read Cain's answer to God's question in verse 9. What becomes increasingly clear about the man Cain?

_____

_____

_____

_____

The Blood of Abel

In verse 10, the word "blood" is mentioned for the first time in Scripture. Abel's blood cried out to the Lord. It seemed alive. Although Abel had been murdered, somehow his life had not been completely snuffed out. Throughout the rest of Scripture, blood will have potent meaning for man's life, both natural and supernatural. It will come to represent the life of man, and, liturgically, the means of atonement for man's sin. "For the life of the flesh is in the blood; . . . it is the blood that makes atonement, by reason of the life" (Lev. 17:11). At the Last Supper, Christ said, "This cup which is poured out for you is the new covenant in my blood" (Lk. 22:20). In the Book of Revelation, the final victory over the devil was won "by the blood of the Lamb" (Rev. 12:11). Thus, we have a consistent witness to the vitality of blood in Scripture, beginning with Abel's blood crying out from the ground.

What do we think Abel's blood said when it cried out to the Lord? Sometimes we think that Abel's blood must have been crying out for justice, which is a reasonable deduction. Yet, because Abel was a righteous man who had faith in God, is it possible that he was crying out for mercy for his brother? In Hebrews 12:24, there is a reference to the blood of Abel, comparing it to the blood of Jesus. The writer of Hebrews says that the blood of the New Covenant speaks "more graciously" than the blood of Abel. The possible implication is that Abel's blood spoke graciously—that is, it gave more than what was deserved. If Abel's blood spoke graciously, then it must have been asking God to show mercy to his murderer, Cain. The blood of Jesus, who also begged forgiveness for murderers, speaks "more graciously" because He was a willing victim of murder, whereas Abel was an unwilling victim. He had been accosted and killed, without any opportunity to choose life or death.

This is an idea worth pondering. If Cain and Abel represent fallen mankind, making their way through life outside of Eden, their story suggests that among the descendants of Adam and Eve, throughout all the ages of human history, there will be some who respond to God and others who will not. Those whose lives are touched by God are willing to offer their suffering to obtain mercy for those who harden themselves. Think of Jesus on the Cross: "Father, forgive them; for they know not what they do" (Lk. 23:43).

8. Look at Cain's response to the punishment God gave him.
   a. What was completely lacking in Cain's response to God?

_____

_____

_____

_____

   b. What was his primary concern?

_____

_____

_____

_____

We Reap What We Sow

Cain is an example of the moral axiom that will appear over and over in Scripture—we reap what we sow. Adam and Eve wanted autonomy from God, and that's exactly what they got, even to the point of being expelled from Eden. Cain's original problem with God was that he was unwilling to give Him the best of himself or his harvest. God's punishment was that Cain would experience from the earth exactly the treatment he had given God; the ground would be hard and unyielding, just as Cain had been in the offer of grace God extended to him. In addition, his desire to be autonomous and not responsible for his brother would have its fulfillment in his life as a "fugitive and a wanderer on earth" (v. 14). His covenant-breaking act would result in him being away from his home and family, God's covenant-keeping community.

Cain's punishment suggests that the worst that can happen to us in life, when we are in rebellion against God, is for Him to give us what we want. If we insist on having life on our own terms, God will give it to us. We will make our own misery.

9. Why do you think God marked Cain so no one would kill him?

_____

_____

_____

_____

10. After the Fall in Eden, we saw signs of God's continued tender care of His creatures. During this second episode of human rebellion, do you see similar signs of God's love for humans?

_____

_____

_____

_____

Two Cultures Develop

🖎 **Read Gen. 4:17–26**

11. Cain departed from the presence of the Lord and began a family. [Note: The question often arises: whom did Cain marry? Pope Pius XII teaches in his encyclical *Humani Generis* that all men are descended from a single human ancestor—Adam and his wife, Eve. Thus, it is reasonable to think that Cain must have married his sister or other relative.] Among his descendants, seventh in line from Adam through Cain, was Lamech.

    a. What type of man does Lamech appear to have been?

_____

_____

_____

_____

    b. What does this suggest about the kind of civilization that developed among people who lived "away from the presence of the LORD"? (v. 16).

_____

_____

_____

_____

12. What was different about the line of descendants of Adam through Seth (v. 26)?

_____

_____

_____

_____

Summary of Genesis 5

The next chapter in Genesis begins with a genealogy of Adam through Seth, the son God gave him to replace the slain Abel. In the first verses, however, there is a beautiful recapitulation of the creation of man, male and female, in the likeness of God (vv. 1–2). The text tells us that Adam "became the father of a son in his own likeness, after his image, and named him Seth" (v. 3). Adam was like God, Adam's son was like his father, and thus Adam passed along to all his human descendants the imprint of divine likeness.

The genealogy of Adam through Seth produced many people, who lived many years. One of the most interesting of his descendants was a man named Enoch, who was seventh in line from Adam through Seth. "Enoch walked with God; and he was not, for God took him" (v. 24). If we look back through Adam's descendants through Cain, we discover that the seventh in that line was Lamech, a proudly violent man, as we have seen. What a contrast in Enoch! He is the first man described as a "prophet" in Scripture (Jude 14–15; cf. Heb. 11:5–6). The difference between Lamech and Enoch helps us understand the difference between the two families of humans who developed through Adam and Eve, typified first by Cain and Abel. There are those who live "away from the presence of the LORD" (4:16), and their lives bear the fruit of that separation, tending towards pride and violence. There are those who "call upon the name of the LORD" (4:26) and respond generously to Him; their lives, too, bear the fruit of that choice.

Enoch is the first biblical example of what we call a "saint"—a human being in whom God does an extraordinary work of His grace. Apparently, he is also the first human to be taken up into heaven (Gen. 5:24; Heb. 11:5). Elijah, the prophet, was another taken that way (2 Kings 2:11), as was the Blessed Virgin Mary. This reference to Enoch, so early in the Scripture, begins the long and wonderful line of humans who walked in the friendship of God.

Genesis 5 also includes the account of another man named Lamech; he was a descendant of Seth. He had a son and "called his name Noah, saying 'Out of the ground which the LORD has cursed this one shall bring us relief from our work and from the toil of our hands'" (v. 29). Lamech's simple statement of hope for his son Noah gave voice to the expectation of the humble human descendants of Adam through Seth that, someday, a male child would grow up to deliver relief from God's curse on sin. Lamech acknowledged the authority of the Lord and did not chafe against the curse. He was not complaining. He was only looking for deliverance. Lamech's hope showed that he was living out God's plan for humanity in the right way; he had a realistic understanding of man's basic predicament, and he clung to exactly the kind of hope that the promise of God in Genesis 3:15 was meant to produce. What a beautiful thing to see!

❧

"Did Not Our Hearts Burn Within Us?"

Our hearts will burn with joy when we consciously open them wide to God's Word. Scripture memorization is a good way to get that started. Here is a suggested memory verse:

If you do well, will you not be accepted? And if you do not do well, sin is couching at the door; its desire is for you, but you must master it.

—Gen. 4:7

Continue to welcome Him into your soul by reflecting on these questions:

In her teachings about sin, the Catholic Church preserves the very serious warning that God gave Cain (Gen. 4:7) and that Saint Paul wrote to the Romans that sin is a form of slavery (6:16). Each time we decide to do the wrong thing, we make it easier for ourselves to do wrong the next time we are tempted. Think about the little sins in your life that you have grown accustomed to. Take seriously God's challenge to Cain, and resolve to turn away from them. Even small sins form calluses on our souls. Ask God to help you find and rid yourself of them.

_____

_____

_____

_____

When you give to God, whether it is time or money, service, attention, or anything else, do you give your best or your leftovers? Consider in your heart what has been given you and what you should return out of thanks to God.

_____

_____

_____

_____

❧

"Stay with Us"

This first lesson on life outside of Eden packs quite a punch. So much of what has characterized human life through all the centuries of our history appears in embryonic form in Genesis 4 and 5. First, there was a mother's announcement of the birth of her son (4:1), a gift from the Lord. The icon of Mother and Son began to take shape. We saw men worshipping God with offerings and that their offerings represented what was in their hearts towards God. Cain and Abel showed us the two kinds of responses that men can have towards their Creator—humility or pride. There was the clear, loving choice God gave to man to choose to live righteously, even after failure.

There was the sober warning that sin begets sin and that resisting it means a battle. Cain became a living example of how sins like jealousy and hatred, if not mortified, give birth to betrayal, lying, and murder. Those sins harden the soul, leaving it callous and impervious to God's approach. We saw that physical death didn't mean the end of a life; Abel was still able to "speak" through his blood. Perhaps his voice was one that cried out for mercy for his brother, true evidence of the righteousness that characterized his life, which had so enraged his brother. We observed God as the loving Father who sought explanations, who punished in order to reform, and who held open the possibility of reconciliation. We recognized the disastrous consequences for human life and development when men live away from the presence of the Lord. We were cheered by the evidence that the descendants of Adam and Eve were still loved deeply by God and that they could, in spite of everything, walk in friendship with Him.

The final scene from Genesis 5, in which Lamech expressed hope for his son Noah, prints indelibly in our minds a conviction that all who love God have shared through the ages. Even among men who acknowledge God—calling upon His Name and responding to His grace, sometimes heroically—there is still the clear understanding that deliverance from God's curse is necessary, that things are not as they should be, either in the earth or in the heart of man. They wait patiently for God to act within human history. Lamech focused that hope on the birth of his son. Thus, the lesson began and ended with a human baby. These chapters perfectly set the stage for the rest of the story of redemption. What we see in outline form here will grow in detail and drama as we wait to see what God has planned for the creation He loves.

Lesson Summary

✔ From the very start, the discord Adam and Eve's sin brought to the world was evident in their children. The internal conflict that would reign between will and emotion was dramatized in the conflict between Cain and Abel: Abel gave God his best while Cain gave only the minimum. Abel's sacrifice pleased God because it reflected a heart of gratitude for God's provision and a desire to please Him. In contrast, the Lord had no regard for Cain's offering because it reflected his heart's desire to keep the best for himself.

✔ Cain's jealousy and anger were apparent to God, who extended an offer to him to set everything right by choosing to live righteously. God warned him that to capitulate to the rage he felt inside would make him subject to sin, like a slave to a master.

✔ Cain chose his way rather than God's. He murdered his brother. God approached him, extending grace to him by calling him to be accountable for his actions. That would have been the first step to forgiveness and restoration. Cain's heart hardened, however. The trap that sin had laid for him snapped shut.

✔ God punished Cain, allowing him to experience in his own life the effects of the choices he had made. His life would be preserved by God, however, perhaps to make reconciliation possible.

✔ Cain left the covenant, which made him a fugitive and wanderer. The civilization that grew from him bore the continuing marks of pride and violence. His descendants became a living picture of human development apart from a humble acknowledgement of God.

✔ Seth, the son born to Adam and Eve to replace Abel, was a man who called on the name of the Lord. Among his descendants, were men like Enoch and Lamech who lived in friendship with God and who patiently waited for deliverance from the curse that rested on man's life because of disobedience.

✔ Noah, whose name means "rest," was a descendant of Seth's. He was so named by his father in the hope that he would be a deliverer of God's people.

For responses to Lesson 8 Questions, see pp. 132–35.

Noah and the Flood
(Genesis 6–8)

Whenever genealogies appear in Scripture, as they did for the first time in our last lesson, they are meant to signify the passing of time and the unfolding of human history. The story of man, begun in the first chapters of Genesis, is now going to proceed in a way that will spread out in many directions. What was it like when the family of man began to fill the earth? We know from the account of Cain and Abel that the human story is going to be marked by violence and tragedy, as well as by faith and hope. These two men are examples of how differently each of the descendants of Adam and Eve will respond to God. Abel loved God; Cain loved himself. Cain murdered his brother, an act that was the fruition of his rebellion against God. His hard, unyielding heart, revealed first in his inadequate offering to God, eventually turned against his brother. His departure from the presence of the Lord meant that his descendants would live and develop away from the light of the truth and the covenant God had made with Adam and Eve. Among Cain's descendants, we noted, was arrogance and violence.

Seth, however, was a son given to Eve to replace the murdered Abel. He was a man who called on the Lord's name, a covenant-keeping man. His descendants showed faithful obedience and friendship with God.

We discovered in Genesis 5 that men were waiting for a deliverer. Even in this ancient era in the story of man, a picture begins to take shape of men who know that they are justly under sin's curse and who are waiting for a male offspring to make some kind of difference for them. Remember Lamech naming his son "Noah," a name that means "rest."

In this lesson, we will watch the further development of man's history, formed out of the two lines of descendants from Cain and Seth. How will the violence and pride of Cain's line coexist with the covenant-keeping of Seth's line? Why does God send such a devastating flood upon the earth? God has shown Himself to be remarkably patient and unconquerably loving to His human creatures. Will this continue?

*[**Note:** This lesson will cover three chapters of Genesis; Genesis 7 will be summarized, without any specific questions to answer.]*

❧

"He Opened to Us the Scriptures"

Before we read God's Word, we ought to take a moment to humble ourselves before Him, remembering that His Word is primarily a conversation with us, not a textbook. "Speak, Lord, for thy servant hears" (1 Sam. 3:10) can be the prayer on our lips. Then, read all the way through Genesis 6–8. Think about what you understand and what you don't understand. Make a simple response to God in terms of what you do understand. Write your prayer in this space:

_____

_____

_____

_____

_____

Now, ask for His help as you work on the questions below.
(Prayer hint: *"Lord, let me not forget that my choice to sin grieves Your heart."*)

❧

Questions
Wickedness Reigns on Earth

❧ **Read Gen. 6:1–10**

The first four verses of Genesis 6 are notoriously difficult to interpret conclusively. Some of the difficulty is removed, however, by determining who the "sons of God" and "the daughters of men" were. We know that there were at least two lines of human development from Adam and Eve, one through Seth and one through Cain. If Seth's descendants were those who called on the name of the Lord, and Cain's were those who lived independently of God, then it is possible that "the sons of God" were male descendents of Seth and the "daughters of men" were female descendents of Cain.[1]

It appears that intermarriage between the two human communities led to a weakening of goodness on earth. Instead of the faith of the one group lifting up the other, wickedness and evil imagination prevailed. Throughout Scripture, there are sober warnings about marriage between people of faith and people without faith or those with false religion. In the history of Israel, one of the greatest dangers the nation faced was the threat presented when Israelites married idolatrous women. Likewise, in the

---

[1] For a helpful discussion of this verse, see Scott Hahn, *A Father Who Keeps His Promises* (Ann Arbor, MI: Servant, 1998), 81–83.

New Testament, Saint Paul speaks specifically against marriage between a believer and an unbeliever (2 Cor. 6:14–16). Because human nature is frail and prone to sin, a marriage between a believer and an unbeliever introduces the possibility of a weakened commitment to keeping God's covenant in the believer. If the unbeliever is the wife, as it seems to be the case here in Genesis, the danger is even greater, since she is the one who will nurture children in that family. The Catholic Church continues to guide Christians away from mixed marriages (*Catechism,* nos. 1633–34). In the case of early human civilization, it is possible that mixed marriages led to a widespread collapse of righteousness on the earth.

The Hebrew of verse 3 is difficult to translate. God said His Spirit would not abide or "strive" with man forever, indicating a kind of withdrawal from him because "he is flesh." That meant that men were living according to their disordered natures. The reference to one hundred and twenty years could mean either the length of time before God withdrew from men, as He did in the Flood, or a reference to a shorter life span in man; the former is most probable. Likewise, it is hard to translate the word "*Nephilim*" with certainty. It can mean "giant" or "tyrant." It has within its possible range of meaning "separated ones." It could be a reference to men who, like Cain, left the covenant of God. In that case, it is perhaps describing those who became notorious ("of renown") for their aggression and presumption, as we saw in the case of Lamech in Genesis 4:23–24.

1. Look at verse 6. This description of God is anthropomorphic, which means the ancient writer described God as if He were a man. We must not understand it to mean that God thought He made a terrible mistake in making man.

a. Read verses 11–13 in the next section. What was it that caused God such grief over men?

_____

_____

_____

_____

b. *Challenge question:* God's intention was to blot out every living thing except Noah, his family, and the animals in the ark (7:4, 21–23). Think about what you have seen in God's reaction to sin thus far in Genesis. He did not blot out Adam and Eve; He did not blot out Cain. But now, He would blot out almost all living things. What do you think is the significance of this?

_____

_____

_____

_____

2. *Challenge question:* Why do you suppose the animals and creeping things were included in God's plan of punishment? (Read also Rom. 8:19–23.)

_____

_____

_____

_____

3. Noah found favor in God's eyes. He was a righteous man. Think for a moment what a statement like this represents about the man Noah. Human society had become so corrupted by wickedness that God wanted to blot man out, but Noah lived righteously in their midst. Read Hebrews 11:1–3, 7. Describe the kind of person you picture Noah to have been.

_____

_____

_____

_____

The World Saved through Noah
Read Gen. 6:11–22

4. Verses 11–12 reveal how completely evil had covered the earth. Yet God found one righteous man and planned to save the world, humans and animals, through him.

a. What does this suggest about God's knowledge of men as distinct individuals? (See Mt. 10:29–31.)

_____

_____

_____

_____

b. What does this suggest about the power of one righteous life?

_____

_____

_____

_____

Summary of Genesis 7

Genesis 7 recalls the onset of the Flood. Although brief, it helps us understand that the destruction of life on earth and the preservation of Noah, his family, and the animals were God's plan to restore His creation to its original destiny. In the early verses of the chapter, we see many references to the number seven. Remember that this number had covenantal significance for the ancient Hebrews. God's hallowing of the seventh day of creation sealed all of the universe into a covenant of love with Him. The covenant was fractured by man's disobedience, but the repeated appearance of the number seven in the text reminds us that God had not forgotten that covenant.

When the water arrived on earth, it first came from the ground, then the sky (7:11). This helps us remember that the primordial earth was also watered from the ground and from the sky (Gen. 2:4–6). The earth was completely covered by water (7:19). This reminds us of how everything began in the first chapter of Genesis—the Spirit of God hovered over the face of the waters (Gen. 1:2). These parallels to the creation story show us that God was undertaking a re-creation of the earth and, in a sense, even of man himself. He wanted to renew the covenant. We should not mistake this for just another attempt to get things right. Rather, we are to absorb from all the details that evoke the creation that God desired to free man from his problems. God's unrelenting initiative in seeking to restore man to his original destiny is unequivocal proof of His love for us. The enormity of God's persistent love should rise up above all the details of man's early history as the sun rises in the morning sky. We dare not interpret any of it apart from the illumination of that bright light. Behind, above, beneath, before, and throughout everything is the glorious love of God for mere mortals. "O LORD, our Lord, how majestic is thy Name in all the earth!" (Ps. 8:9).

The Waters Subside
🖋 **Read Gen. 8:1–12**

5. Noah and his family had to wait quite awhile before they could leave the ark.
   a. If God had miraculously made the waters appear, what question might they have legitimately asked while they waited for the waters to disappear?

_____
_____
_____
_____

   b. *Challenge question:* Why do you think God just let nature take its course?

_____
_____
_____
_____

Noah's Ark

The ark that Noah was to build was going to be the means of salvation for Noah, his family, and the animals taken into it. It was going to be roomy and well-stocked with food. The door to the ark would be in its side. God would make a covenant with everything inside of it. It was going to ride through water to safety.

The Fathers of the early Church saw the ark as a figure of the Church. Saint Augustine writes:

God ordered Noah to build an ark in which he and his family would escape from the devastation of the flood. Undoubtedly the ark is a symbol of the City of God on pilgrimage in this world, that is, a symbol of the Church which was saved by the wood on which there hung the Mediator between God and men—Christ Jesus, himself a man. Even the measurements of length, height and breadth of the ark are a symbol of the human body in which He came. [. . .] The door open in the side of the ark surely symbolizes the open wound made by the lance in the side of the Crucified—the door by which those who come to him enter in the sense that believers enter the Church by means of the sacraments which issued from that wound."[2]

6. Read verses 6–12. Think of the picture of the dove going back and forth from the ark, looking for habitable land.

a. Eventually, the dove did not return (v. 12). What did that mean to Noah?

_____

_____

_____

_____

b. *Challenge question:* Read Matthew 3:16–17 and the Catechism, no. 701. What meaning does the Church help us to see in the Gospel scene when the Holy Spirit descended "like a dove" on Jesus?

_____

_____

_____

_____

"Go Forth from the Ark"

🎜 **Read Gen. 8:13–22**

7. Look at the command God gave Noah in verse 17. Read also Genesis 1:28. What does this language, so reminiscent of creation, help us to understand about the meaning of this moment when Noah and his family came out of the ark?

_____

_____

_____

_____

8. Look at the very first thing Noah did when he got off the ark (v. 20).
a. What was it?

_____

_____

_____

_____

---

[2] Saint Augustine, *De civitate Dei*, bk.15, chap. 26, as quoted in *The Navarre Bible: Pentateuch*, (Princeton, NJ: Scepter Publishers, 1999), 70.

b. Why do you suppose this act pleased the Lord greatly?

_____

_____

_____

_____

Incense at Mass

The Lord was pleased with the smell of Noah's sacrifice (8:21) because of what it represented. The aroma was an expression of Noah's gratitude and worship. In the Mass, whenever incense is used, we reproduce this moment of pleasure for God. The smell of the incense represents our act of worship and praise, as we offer up the perfect sacrifice of thanksgiving—ourselves and the Eucharist.

c. _Challenge question:_ Remember that Noah's name meant "rest." Read verses 21–22. Did Noah live up to his name?

_____

_____

_____

_____

"Did Not Our Hearts Burn Within Us?"

Our hearts will burn with joy when we consciously open them wide to God's Word. Scripture memorization is a good way to get that started. Here is a suggested memory verse.

> _Then Noah built an altar to the LORD, and took of every clean animal and of every clean bird, and offered burnt offerings on the altar. And when the LORD smelled the pleasing odor, the LORD said in his heart, "I will never again curse the ground because of man, for the imagination of man's heart is evil from his youth; neither will I ever again destroy every living creature as I have done."_
>
> —_Gen. 8:20–21_

Continue to welcome Him into your soul by reflecting on these questions:

Noah was a man who was unaffected by the great wickedness around him. He remained faithful to the ways of God. We recognize this as a difficult thing to do, because our human nature, even after Baptism, is still bent in the direction of sin. Take the time to examine yourself to see if you are being influenced for bad instead of for good by the people around you. Perhaps you are not being dragged into great wickedness, but do others make it easier for you to gossip, to complain, to be dishonest, to be too attached to worldly possessions, to neglect your spiritual life, etc.? If so, build an ark to protect yourself. That should include confession, resolve, self-discipline, and prayer. Ask Noah to pray for you to live as a bright light in your world.

_____

_____

_____

_____

There are no unobserved moments in a Christian's life. Think about how this truth can both save you from danger and give you the deepest possible joy. Be specific.

_____

_____

_____

_____

Noah had to wait patiently for the waters of judgment and devastation to recede. Is there a place in your life now where you must do the same? Is there anything in this lesson that will help your waiting to lead to holiness in you?

_____

_____

_____

_____

⚡

"Stay with Us"

When you read the account of the Flood, realizing that everyone except Noah's family died because of God's judgment, did you have a twinge of wondering if that was fair? After all, if some human civilizations developed away from the covenant-keepers, thus becoming intensely evil, perhaps we want to say that they didn't know any better. Maybe we think they never really had a chance to live their lives the way Noah did.

Saint Paul, in his Epistle to the Romans, helps us to better understand just exactly what was going on among men whose lives were given over to wickedness. It is worth examining what he has to say in the first chapter of that letter:

> For the wrath of God is revealed from heaven against all ungodliness and wickedness of men who by their wickedness suppress the truth. For what can be known about God is plain to them, because God has shown it to them. Ever since the creation of the world his invisible nature, namely, his eternal power and deity, has been clearly perceived in the things that have been made. So they are without excuse; for although they knew God they did not honor him as God or give thanks to him, but they became futile in their thinking and their senseless minds were darkened. Claiming to be wise, they became fools, and exchanged the glory of the immortal God for images resembling mortal man or birds or animals or reptiles.

Therefore God gave them up in the lusts of their hearts to impurity, to the dishonoring of their bodies among themselves, because they exchanged the truth about God for a lie and worshiped and served the creature rather than the Creator, who is blessed for ever! Amen. (vv. 18–24)

Here we see that Saint Paul says that anyone who lives on the planet Earth, whether he lives among covenant-keeping people or not, knows enough about God to live in the right way. Why? Because God has revealed Himself in His works. Looking around at the world in which he lives, a man is capable of recognizing that (1) there is a God, (2) He is powerful, and (3) He deserves to be honored and thanked (Rom. 1:20–21). When a man chooses not to act on what he knows to be true, he suppresses truth itself. It isn't that he has been deprived of it—he simply refuses to live by it.

When that happens, things go downhill fast. As Saint Paul tells us:

And since they did not see fit to acknowledge God, God gave them up to a base mind and to improper conduct. They were filled with all manner of wickedness, evil, covetousness, malice. Full of envy, murder, strife, deceit, malignity, they are gossips, slanderers, haters of God, insolent, haughty, boastful, inventors of evil, disobedient to parents, foolish, faithless, heartless, ruthless. Though they know God's decree that those who do such things deserve to die, they not only do them but approve those who practice them. (Rom. 1:28–32)

This is a description of what happened in the early history of man and what continues to happen when men, like Cain, know what is right to do but refuse to do it. When that happens, the most merciful thing God can do is to punish them. It is often only when men are faced with suffering and death that their autonomy crumbles to ash, and they are willing to cry out to God, whom they are finally ready to acknowledge as the only One who can help.

The Flood was just such an occasion. It was the just, merciful response of God to the mess man had made for himself. We may ask, suppose some people, as the waters of the Flood overwhelmed them, cried out to God for mercy? What if, in the very last seconds of their lives, they repented of their great offense against God? Saint Peter, in 1 Peter 3:18–22, tells us more about the Flood, lest we have any misgivings:

For Christ also died for sins once for all, the righteous for the unrighteous, that he might bring us to God, being put to death in the flesh but made alive in the spirit; in which he went and preached to the spirits in prison, who formerly did not obey, when God's patience waited in the days of Noah, during the building of the ark, in which a few, that is, eight persons, were saved through water. Baptism, which corresponds to this, now saves you, not as a removal of dirt from the body but as an appeal to God for a clear conscience, through the resurrection of Jesus Christ, who has gone into heaven and is at the right hand of God, with angels, authorities, and powers subject to him.

The Church tells us that "Christ went down into the depths of death so that 'the dead will hear the voice of the Son of God, and those who hear will live'" (*Catechism,* no. 635). When Jesus entered "the depths of death" to preach the Good News of salvation, if there were any who had been humbled by the Flood, even in the last moments of consciousness, surely they responded to Him. But those who, like Cain, had hardened their hearts through sin might well have had the same reaction to Christ as Cain had to God—"Thanks, but no thanks." We should never worry about the justice and fairness of God (see *Catechism,* nos. 632–35).

Lesson Summary

✔ Over time, and possibly as a result of intermarriage between men who called on the name of the Lord and women who did not, great wickedness spread throughout the human community on earth. There was unchecked violence and evil imagination everywhere.

✔ God decided to judge this wickedness by sending a great flood to blot out all living things. There was, however, one man who still lived the way God intended men to live—Noah. He found favor in God's sight.

✔ The righteous man, Noah, was to build an ark to preserve some life—that of his family and of the animals God instructed him to carry into it. He obeyed and prepared for the onslaught.

✔ The earth returned to a time of watery chaos as a result of God's judgment. Because of language evocative of the first creation story, we recognized in this account that God was re-creating the earth and man's life in order to cleanse it from the great evil that pervaded it.

✔ When God caused the waters to subside, a dove became the symbol that the earth was ready to receive renewed life upon it.

✔ As soon as he was off the ark, Noah made an offering to the Lord. This act deeply pleased God (as the wickedness had deeply grieved Him). He made a promise never to repeat this kind of judgment on the earth in the history of man. Noah's obedience and reverence was the human agency of God's blessing on the earth and "rest" for troubled man.

For responses to Lesson 9 Questions, see pp. 135–37.

The Covenant Renewed
(Genesis 9–11)

In some ways, for people closely studying the early chapters of Genesis, the story of the Flood comes as a kind of catharsis. Rebellion in and out of Eden, the spread of wickedness throughout the earth, and the profound sadness that comes from knowing how all this grieved God does make us want to cry out for an end to it all, and for a fresh start. In the account of Noah, who was a human being who still loved God more than he loved himself, we had reason to breathe a sigh of relief and hope. Perhaps with the earth washed clean of violence and with the continuation of human life through a righteous man and his family, we can expect better things. Surely the scene from Genesis 8 gave us some basis for this hope. God was once again pleased by what He saw on earth (an echo of the "very good" of the first creation); He took delight in the aroma of Noah's sacrifice.

Genesis 6–8, with the frequent use of language evocative of the first creation, prepares us to expect to see a renewal of the covenant that God graciously made with all creation at its beginning. We expect that He will make it clear how He wants life on the renewed planet to be lived. And because God is Goodness itself, we are counting on some demonstration of His deep, abiding, persistent love for man—the kind of love we have already seen in our study, which reaches down to man in his dependent, helpless condition and gives so much more than he deserves. We will not be disappointed.

That is, we won't be disappointed in God. But what about the humans? It's hard for us to forget that the problem in Eden was man's doing. Were men's hearts also washed clean by the Flood?

"He Opened to Us the Scriptures"

Before we read God's Word, we ought to take a moment to humble ourselves before Him, remembering that His Word is primarily a conversation with us, not a textbook.

"Speak, Lord, for thy servant hears" (1 Sam. 3:10) can be the prayer on our lips. Then, read all the way through Genesis 9–11. Think about what you understand and what you don't understand. Make a simple response to God in terms of what you do understand. Write your prayer in this space:

_____

_____

_____

_____

_____

Now, ask for His help as you work on the questions below.
(Prayer hint: *"Lord, help me to make the most of every fresh start You give me."*)

Questions
A Blessing from God

Read Gen. 9:1–7
Read Genesis 1:28–31 and Genesis 9:1–7. These two scenes are very similar, which is not a coincidence.

a. What do you think we are meant to understand by this similarity?

_____

_____

_____

b. *Challenge question:* There is a dramatic difference between these two scenes: the second one is punctuated by fear and dread. What does that help us to understand about the re-creation?

_____

_____

_____

_____

2. Recall that in Genesis 4, Cain feared that someone would kill him because he murdered Abel, his brother. Yet God preserved his life. In the renewed world, those who kill others will lose their lives. What do you think explains this change?

_____

_____

_____

_____

3. In verse 4, God prohibited eating the flesh of animals that had any blood in it. Why do you think that God announced this strong taboo on blood?

_____

_____

_____

_____

Capital Punishment and Genesis 9:6

How can we reconcile God's declaration of capital punishment for murder, recorded here in Genesis 9, with the tireless campaign of Pope John Paul II, in his pontificate, against it? The *Catechism* tells us:

> Assuming that the guilty party's identity and responsibility have been fully determined, the traditional teaching of the Church does not exclude recourse to the death penalty, if this is the only possible way of effectively defending human lives against the unjust aggressor.
>
> If, however, non-lethal means are sufficient to defend and protect people's safety from the aggressor, authority will limit itself to such means, as these are more in keeping with the concrete conditions of the common good and more in conformity with the dignity of the human person.
>
> Today, in fact, as a consequence of the possibilities which the state has for effectively preventing crime, by rendering one who has committed an offense incapable of doing harm—without definitively taking away from him the possibility of redeeming himself—the cases in which the execution of the offender is an absolute necessity "are very rare, if not practically non-existent" (*Catechism*, no. 2267, quoting *Evangelium Vitae* 56).

The Church teaches that for much of human history, beginning with Noah, executing certain kinds of criminals was the only way to protect society against them. Now, however, in the modern era with its penal institutions, some societies are capable of curbing violence without killing those guilty of it. Pope John Paul II has been a strong voice speaking out against capital punishment in those societies because of his unwavering commitment to the dignity and sacredness of human life, even when men sin greatly. As God says here in this passage: "God made man in His own image" (Gen. 9:6). If, by imprisonment, we can protect society and prevent danger from a criminal, we should not take his life. Governments should respect life, not taking it unnecessarily. Further, they can aim to rehabilitate criminals to live a more productive life, while the Church prays for their repentance, conversion, and reconciliation with God.

The Sign of the Covenant

🦌 **Read Gen. 9:8–17**

4. God made a covenant with Noah and his sons. (A covenant is an agreement between parties that creates a family relationship among them.) God promised that He would never again destroy all life on the earth again with a flood. His just wrath had been spent. There was no need to fear any further destruction. God told Noah that the rainbow would represent this covenant promise.

a. In the rainbow, God closely identified Himself with something beautiful in the sky. What potential risk did God take when He chose to use a rainbow as the covenant sign?

_____

_____

_____

_____

b. *Challenge question:* Why do you think God took that risk? (See also *Catechism,* no. 1146.)

_____

_____

_____

_____

God and the Rainbow

In the Garden of Eden, everything that existed—trees, animals, fruit, sun, sky, moon—gave testimony to Adam and Eve that God exists and that He is good. In the re-creation, God chose one element in creation, the rainbow, to restore man's confidence in His goodness and power. How? He told Noah that whenever the rainbow appeared in the heavens, He would do something: "When the bow is in the clouds, I will look upon it and remember the everlasting covenant between God and every living creature" (9:16). This made the rainbow much more than a sign. If it had been only a sign, God would have told Noah, "When the bow is in the clouds, remember the covenant." The rainbow would have reminded Noah to do something. Instead, when the bow appeared, God committed Himself to doing something on behalf of every living creature. He would do the remembering.

In this, God used an ordinary element in nature to do an extraordinary thing for man. This is what the Church calls a sacrament. God does a gracious work for man in conjunction with an element in nature—bread, wine, water, oil. The rainbow was the first "sacrament" of the re-creation.

The Sons of Noah

🔥 **Read Gen. 9:18–29**

5. Read verse 20. Noah was a gardener (of a vineyard) who abused the fruit he had there. What kind of warning do you think this might be?

_____

_____

_____

_____

*[**Note:** It is difficult to know precisely the nature of Ham's offense against his father in 9:22. In Leviticus 18:7–16, we see that the phrase "uncover nakedness" had sexual meaning for the Hebrews. (In the New American Catholic Bible, these words are translated as "have sexual intercourse.") In Leviticus 18:7–8, we read: "You shall not uncover the nakedness of your father, which is the nakedness of your mother; she is your mother, you shall not uncover her nakedness. You shall not uncover the nakedness of your father's wife; it is your father's nakedness." Could the nakedness of Noah be a reference to his wife's nakedness? This is quite possibly a reference to incest on the part of Ham. In addition, when Noah awoke from sleep and realized what happened, he cursed Canaan, the son of Ham. This suggests that the discovery of pregnancy in Noah's wife and perhaps the birth of the son of the incestuous union was the occasion for Noah's curse on that child, Canaan. This explains why the son and not the father was cursed. Canaan would have had an unlawful relationship with Noah.]*

6. What kind of son did Ham appear to be (v. 22)?

_____

_____

_____

_____

7. What strength of character did Shem and Japheth show (v. 23)?

_____

_____

_____

_____

*[**Note:** The Revised Standard Version–Catholic Edition translation of Genesis 9:26 is not as accurate as it could be. A better rendering of that verse is "Blessed be the Lord, the God of Shem." This is the first time in the Bible that God is identified with the name of a man. As Noah's firstborn son, Shem, was set in a position of superiority over his brothers. In fact, the son of Ham, Canaan, was destined to serve as a "slave" to Shem. In other words, the Canaan-ites were to be subordinate to the Shem-ites (whom we call now "Semites"). Noah said that God would "dwell in the tents of Shem," suggesting a close and blessed relationship between the Shemites and God. This blessing and curse helps us understand the later troubled relationship between the Israelites (Semites) and the Canaanites, who fought for possession of Shem's ancestral inheritance of land.]*

Summary of Genesis 10

The picture in Genesis 10 is one of slow but steady repopulation of the earth. As the *Catechism* says, "After the unity of the human race was shattered by sin, God at once sought to save humanity part by part. The covenant with Noah after the flood gives expression to the principle of the divine economy toward the 'nations,' in other words, toward men grouped 'in their lands, each with [its] own language, by their families, in their nations [Gen. 10:5; cf. 9:9–10, 16; 10:20–31]'" (no. 56).

Because all humans have descended from Noah and his family, we are reminded that the human community is really a family. We knew this at the time of the creation, and we are seeing it again here. The longing that men have for universal peace, the end to wars, and respect for human life stems from this deep awareness that we are all related to each other and ought to live together in familial peace. In addition, of course, all men are God's children, even when their national religions have lost much of the truth about God that Noah and his family would have possessed. As the family of man spread out over the earth and through the centuries, various cultures may have preserved elements of some truths about God even as they lost others. With additions and subtractions, with distortions and misunderstandings, those elements could have become the basis for various religions of the world. It is not difficult to imagine a process like that—a fracturing of the covenant story handed down through Noah's generation. The Church teaches that many non-Christian religions contain some of these elements of truth; it is the Christian Gospel and the teaching of the Church that give men the possibility of knowing and experiencing the fullness of the truth (*Catechism,* nos. 842–45).

Of special interest to us in this chapter is Nimrod (10:8–11), who was a descendant of Ham through Cush. He is described as one who gained a certain ascendancy and was mighty "before the LORD." This phrase is not meant to suggest that he had a great relationship with the Lord. Rather, it is used to express the degree of his notoriety. It is reminiscent of "the mighty ones" who were on the earth at the time of the Flood (6:4). Thus, Nimrod's reputation would have been one of great might, not goodness. He was the founder of the first Mesopotamian kingdom and the civilizations that became known as Assyria and Babylonia. This is the first place in the Bible where the term "kingdom" occurs. It suggests the start of nations that were characterized by prideful opposition to the Lord (Gen. 11:1–9; cf. Rev. 17:1–18).

The Tower of Babel

⚡ **Read Gen. 11:1–9**

8. Nimrod, a descendant of Ham, built the city of Babel (Gen. 10:10).

a. What appears to have been the motivation of this city's builders, especially in the creation of the tower?

_____
_____
_____
_____

[Note: Interestingly, these descendants of Ham wanted to make a "name" for themselves. The word for "name" in Hebrew was "shem." This desire to make their own "name" may indicate that they were consciously rejecting their ancestral subordination to Shem and his descendants, undoing the blessing and cursing of their patriarch, Noah.]

b. What threat to mankind did God see in their building project?

_____
_____
_____
_____

c. *Challenge question:* The solution to this offense in Babel was for God to fragment human civilization by different languages. What then, does the diversity in human language really represent? (See also *Catechism,* no. 57.)

_____
_____
_____
_____

The Descendants of Shem

Read Gen. 11:10–32

[Note: These verses give the genealogy of Shem, Noah's righteous firstborn son. See that Shem lived a very long time, long enough to be alive when Abram was born. That would have made Shem the great patriarch of Noah's family and the one on whom the blessing of God rested.]

9. This genealogy leads up to one family, Terah, and his sons, Abram and Nahor. They lived in Ur, a large city of Mesopotamia. Read Joshua 24:2–4. What had become of Shem's "family religion" by this time?

_____
_____
_____
_____

10. *Challenge question:* Think about how the civilization of man developed from Noah and his sons. Although Noah was a righteous, faithful man, his drunkenness made him vulnerable to an outrage by one of his sons. He had to put some of his own descendants under a curse. As the sons of Noah had families, there were some who gained reputations for all the wrong reasons. This all looks strangely familiar. Did the re-creation of the earth work?

_____
_____
_____
_____

What Happens Next?

As we conclude our study of this section of Genesis, it is appropriate to ask, "What happens next?" The best way to prepare for the answer to that question is to ask two more: (1) what has happened already? and (2) what needs to happen next? We have already seen something of a pattern develop, in just eleven chapters of Genesis. We have recognized, in an unmistakable way, that God desired the existence of human creatures on earth so that He could share His life with them. Made in His image and likeness, with a vocation that matched His, man and woman were truly the crown of God's creation. However, they abused their freedom and rebelled against Him. Although they experienced severe punishment for their disobedience, they discovered (and so did we) that there was a "deeper magic" at work in the universe (as Aslan, the Lion in C. S. Lewis' *The Lion, the Witch, and the Wardrobe*, once said about Narnia). God did not give up on His plan for humanity. Once man and woman stepped out of Eden, God began His relentless hunt to return them to Paradise, their true home.

Just as we have seen a pattern of God's goodness in Genesis 1–11, so we have seen a pattern of human weakness and failure. A massive expansion of wickedness on earth precipitated God's judgment in the Flood; one man's righteousness saved the human race from it. Before long, however, God had to visit the earth in judgment again, striking down a tower built by men who were attempting to storm heaven. He confused the one language that had made it possible for men to use their unity for all the wrong purposes.

Still, we know that God had a future for humanity. We know that plan included a woman and her seed, who would turn the tide in a cosmic battle. We know that God desired to bless, not curse, His human family. Even though Adam and Eve were expelled from the Garden, the memory of the blessedness there would always beckon to their descendants.

So, what needs to happen next? We need to see more of God's plan for His creation. We need to know how He will overcome the persistent pattern of man's weakness and sin, which overpowered goodness wherever it existed. How would God contain man's rebellion, as nations developed and expanded over the earth? Before the Flood, one man's righteousness countered the evil intent of many hearts. After the Flood, will one nation's righteousness make a difference in all that had gone wrong on earth?

The answer to that question lies in our study of the next section of Genesis, *God and His Family* (Gen. 12–50).

"Did Not Our Hearts Burn Within Us?"

Our hearts will burn with joy when we consciously open them wide to God's Word. Scripture memorization is a good way to get that started. Here is a suggested memory verse:

And God said, "This is the sign of the covenant which I make between me and you and every living creature that is with you, for all future generations: I set my bow in the cloud, and it shall be a sign of the covenant between me and the earth."

—Gen. 9:12–13

Continue to welcome Him into your soul by reflecting on these questions:

Sometimes Catholics are accused by others of caring more about the outward forms of sacraments than about the direct encounter with Jesus that they are meant to give. This shows up in people who would never miss Mass, who go to Confession, who have all their children baptized and confirmed, but who seem not to have a living, vital relationship with God. If they are people who do not exhibit the fruit of the Spirit in their lives—such as kindness, self-control, and especially charity—then they appear to outsiders as people who could gaze on a rainbow and not meet the God who set it in the sky. Would anyone be able to say that of you? It is always good for our souls to check to see if we have fallen into ritual presumption. If we love the sacraments, our lives should bear the fruit of divine encounters. Ask God to help you be honest with Him about this today. Perhaps He has a word for you.

_____

_____

_____

_____

Look around your world today. Even if you don't see a rainbow in the sky, what is there in your line of vision that is a powerful reminder of who God is and how much He loves you? Thank Him for it.

_____

_____

_____

_____

"Stay with Us"

Did you feel disappointed when Noah, a man so bright in faith and obedience, succumbed to drunkenness, which led to something even darker? In the bleak wasteland of a world given over to evil, Noah seemed like a man we could trust. He looked like a hero.

Why is it so difficult to accept flawed heroes? Is it because all humans long for a *perfect* human, one who will not disappoint us and let our dreams die? Ever since Adam, we have been looking for one who won't botch things up. We want to see a human be all that God meant for us to be.

The characters of the Old Testament, such as Adam and Abel and Noah, begin to prepare us for just such a Person. Even though humans in the story of the Old

Testament disappoint us from time to time, we should never let their humanity sour us or tempt us to be contemptuous of them. We must never forget that God's promise in Genesis 3:15 to defeat His enemy *through* humans means that in this battle, step by step, God's work will have a human face on it. This is the magnificent condescension of God to man. It is also God's resounding confirmation that He did not make a mistake in creating man. God knows very well what weaknesses beset humanity. Nevertheless, He works relentlessly to make sure that someday our dream of human perfection will be a reality, not a dream. To be a Christian means not being squeamish about human beings doing divine work. This is especially true for Catholics, because sometimes our Protestant brethren protest that we have too many "mere humans" in our understanding of redemption. We have Mary, "just a woman," as Queen of Heaven and Mother of the Church. We have a pope, "only a man," who sits in the line of Peter and holds the keys of the kingdom. We have saints, men and women who are "just like us," to serve as our examples and advocates in their lives as God's friends. When this charge is raised against us, we should bow our heads, give thanks to God, and smile deeply in our souls. A "human" Church? Exactly.

Lesson Summary

✔ When Noah and his family got off the ark, God blessed them and gave them a command to be fruitful and multiply. Although the earth and life on it underwent a renewal, there was still evidence that men were not as they had once been in Eden. The dread that animals would experience toward man would be a sign of the loss of that harmony.

✔ Man was to respect the blood of every living thing, even that of animals, because it is a sign of life, a gift from God. God instituted a law of capital punishment for murder in order to keep in check the violence in man's nature that too easily overwhelms the good.

✔ God established a covenant with Noah and his family, promising to never again destroy all life on the earth or disrupt its order by a flood. He used an element in nature, the rainbow, to seal this promise.

✔ Noah became drunk in his vineyard, making it possible for his second son, Ham, to sin against him. Ham lacked respect for his father, reflecting in him a spirit of insubordination and rebellion. This was evidence that although God had renewed the earth, sin was still present and active in men, wreaking its destruction.

✔ Shem and Japheth, the oldest and youngest brothers, did what they could to rectify Ham's offense. Noah blessed Shem, perhaps indicating his role as an example to his brothers as one who respected and honored his father's dignity.

✔ Noah cursed Canaan, the son of Ham. He and his descendants were to serve Shem and his descendants.

✔ In a city, Babel, built by descendants of Ham, men decided to band together and make a name for themselves, establishing a center of power and autonomy. Their pride led them to try to build a tower to heaven, a demonstration of their insubordination and arrogance.

✔ God opposed this abuse of man's unity by confusing the one language men spoke into many different languages. They had to quit building the city and tower because they could not communicate. The separation of men into nations speaking different languages is a sign that men used their unity for the wrong goals. It would take a miracle of redemption and new birth to give men natures in which they would use their unity to love and serve God. That restoration began on the day of Pentecost and continues today.

For responses to Lesson 10 Questions, see pp. 137–40.

Appendix A

How to Read the First Chapter of Genesis
By George Sim Johnston

The first chapter of Genesis remains a great stumbling block for the modern mind. The average educated person "knows" that the creation account in Genesis is contradicted by what science tells us about the origin of the universe and the animal kingdom. Charles Darwin himself discarded a mild Protestant faith when he concluded that the author of Genesis was a bad geologist. To his mind, the biblical six days of creation and Lyell's *Principles of Geology* could not both be true.

The discomfort with Genesis, moreover, has not been restricted to the educated classes. According to the famous French worker-priest Abbe Michonneau, the apparent conflict between science and the six-day creation account promoted atheism among the poor far more effectively than any social injustice. Darwinian evolution is a major ingredient of that "science." So is the "Big Bang" model of the universe, which plausibly asserts that the cosmos is billions, and not thousands, of years old.

The confusion over this issue, which Pope John Paul II addressed in 1996 in his highly publicized letter about evolution, boils down to the question of how to read the biblical creation account. In his letter, John Paul simply reiterated what the Magisterium has argued tirelessly since Leo XIII's *Providentissimus Deus* (1893): the author of Genesis did not intend to provide a scientific explanation of how God created the world. Unfortunately, there are still biblical fundamentalists, Catholic and Protestant, who do not embrace this point.

When Christ said that the mustard seed was the smallest of seeds—and it is about the size of a speck of dust—He was not laying down a principle of botany. In fact, botanists tell us there are smaller seeds. Our Lord was simply talking to the men of His time in their own language, and with reference to their own experience. Similarly, the Hebrew word for "day" used in Genesis (*yom*) can mean a twenty-four-hour day, or a longer period. Hence the warning of Pius XII in *Divino Afflante*

This article first appeared in *Lay Witness* magazine, published by Catholics United for the Faith. Reprinted with permission.

Spiritu (1943) that the true sense of a biblical passage is not always obvious. The sacred authors wrote in the idioms of their time and place.

As Catholics, we must believe that every word of Scripture is inspired by the Holy Spirit—a claim the Church will not make even for her infallible pronouncements. However, we must not imagine the biblical authors as going into a trance and taking automatic dictation in a "pure" language, untouched by historical contingency. Rather, God made full use of the writers' habits of mind and expression. It's the old mystery of grace and free will.

A modern reader of Genesis must bear in mind the principles of biblical exegesis laid down by Saint Augustine in his great work *De Genesi Ad Litteram* (On the Literal Interpretation of Genesis). Augustine taught that whenever reason established with certainty a *fact* about the physical world, seemingly contrary statements in the Bible must be interpreted accordingly. He opposed the idea of a "Christian account" of natural phenomena in opposition to what could be known by science. He viewed such accounts as "most deplorable and harmful, and to be avoided at any cost," because on hearing them the non-believer "could hardly hold his laughter on seeing, as the saying goes, the error rise sky-high."

As early as AD 410, then, the greatest of the western Church Fathers was telling us that the Book of Genesis is not an astrophysics or geology textbook. Augustine himself was a kind of evolutionist, speculating that God's creation of the cosmos was an instantaneous act whose effects unfolded over a long period. God had planted "rational seeds" in nature which eventually developed into the diversity of plants and animals we see today. Saint Thomas Aquinas cites this view of Augustine's more than once in the course of the *Summa Theologiae*. Saint Thomas, author Etienne Gilson writes,

> was well aware that the Book of Genesis was not a treatise on cosmography for the use of scholars. It was a statement of the truth intended for the simple people whom Moses was addressing. Thus it is sometimes possible to interpret it in a variety of ways. So it was that when we speak of the six days of creation, we can understand by it either six successive days, as do Ambrose, Basil, Chrysostom and Gregory, and is suggested by the letter of the text . . . Or we can with Augustine take it to refer to the simultaneous creation of all beings with days symbolizing the various orders of beings. This second interpretation is at first sight less literal, but is, rationally speaking, more satisfying. It is the one that St. Thomas adopts, although he does not exclude the other which, as he says, can also be held.

In this century, Cardinal Bea, who helped Pius XII draft *Divino Afflante Spiritu,* wrote that Genesis does not deal with the "true constitution of visible things." It is meant to convey truths outside the scientific order.

While they do not teach science, the early chapters of Genesis are history and not myth. But they are not history as it would be written by a modern historian. (It is not as though there was a camcorder in the Garden of Eden.) You might say that they are history written in mythic language—a poetic compression of the truth, as it were. We are obliged to believe the fundamental truths expressed by the sacred author—for example, that our first parents, tempted by the devil, committed a primal act of disobedience whose effects we still suffer (*Catechism*, no. 390). But the Catholic doctrine of original sin is entirely outside the realm of physical science. It's worth keeping in mind, however, Newman's remark that the more he contemplated humanity, the clearer it became to him that the race was "implicated in some terrible aboriginal calamity."[1]

Biblical fundamentalism—and its corollary, creation science—is a distinctly Protestant phenomenon. Although it has roots in the commentaries on Genesis written by Luther and Calvin, its real beginning was in early twentieth century America. Biblical literalism was a defense against the onslaught of rationalist criticism launched by German scholars who were intent on undermining Christian belief in the inerrancy of Scripture. Certain Protestant denominations that were already suspicious of science took refuge in a semantic literalism that sheltered the Bible from the invasive procedures of agnostic scholarship. The intellectual simplicity and doctrinal clarity of this position make it attractive to some Catholics today. This appeal is understandable. They are seeking refuge from the attacks of heterodox theologians who seem as eager as their nineteenth century forebears to deconstruct the faith.

The temptation to biblical literalism should be avoided, however. The Bible was never meant to be read apart from the teaching authority established by Christ. Even many Catholics are not aware of the "Catholic" origins of the Bible. It was not until the end of the fourth century that the twenty-seven books which comprise the New Testament were agreed upon by two Church councils, subject to final approval by the pope. And it was the Church that insisted, against the protests of heretics, that the Old Testament be included in the Christian canon. The Bible was never meant to stand alone as a separate authority. It is the Church, the Mystical Body of Christ, that preserves the deposit of the faith, of which Scripture is an integral part. Saint Augustine, as usual, got it exactly right: "But for the authority of the Catholic Church, I would not believe the Gospel."[2]

Since Leo XIII, the Magisterium has progressively discouraged the literalistic reading of Genesis favored by Protestants. Can a Catholic nonetheless read Genesis as a scientific treatise? Yes, if he wants to—but he may find himself in the dilemma of trying to force scientific data into a biblical template that was never meant to receive it. And he will be severely handicapped in doing apologetics in a post-Christian world. He will, in fact, be the reverse of apostolic if he tries to explain to anyone the doctrine of creation in the terms of ancient Hebrew cosmology.

The test of a first-rate intellect, it has been said, is the ability to hold two seemingly opposed ideas and retain the ability to function. A brilliant twentieth-century Catholic apologist, Frank J. Sheed, wrote of the creation account in his masterpiece, *Theology and Sanity*. His words are an invitation to Catholics tempted by biblical literalism to use their reason and not engage in overly simplistic readings of Scripture. The author of Genesis, Sheed writes,

> tells us of the fact but not the process: there was an assembly of elements of the material universe, but was it instantaneous or spread over a considerable space and time? Was it complete in one act, or by stages? Were those elements, for

---

[1] John Henry Cardinal Newman, "General Answer to Mr. Kingsley," in *Apologia Pro Vita Sua*, part 7.
[2] Saint Augustine, *Contra epistolam Manichaei*, chap. 5, no. 6.

instance, formed into an animal body which as one generation followed another gradually evolved—not, of course, by the ordinary laws of matter but under the special guidance of God—to a point where it was capable of union with a spiritual soul, which God created and infused into it? The statement in Genesis does not seem actually to exclude this, but it certainly does not say it. Nor has the Church formally said that it is not so.[3]

Catholics in reality have no cause to be timid about Scripture or science. They simply need to distinguish between two complementary but distinct orders of knowledge—theological and scientific—and allow each its due competence. They should be extremely cautious about mixing the two. The Magisterium learned this the hard way in the Galileo affair. A faithful Catholic should be calmly anchored in the proposition that truth is indivisible, and the works of God cannot contradict what He has chosen to reveal through Scripture and Tradition.

[3] Frank J. Sheed, *Theology and Sanity* (New York: Sheed and Ward, 1946), 134.

Appendix B

Guide to Lesson Questions

Lesson 1

To make the most of this study, respond to all the questions yourself before reading these responses.

1. a. There are four phrases repeated throughout Genesis 1: (1) "And God said, 'Let there be . . . and it was so,'"(2) "And God saw that it was good," (3) "And there was evening and there was morning," and also (4) "God called . . ."

b. (1) In the repetition of this phrase, we see first the power of God's Word to call things into existence. We see that God is not only powerful, but that He used His power to create life. He is the source of life. (2) In the repetition of this phrase, we see that pleasure and goodness are packed into creation, intensifying until God pronounced it "very good" at the end. In this, we see God's own goodness, which He shared with His creation, and His intention to create the universe to be a source of satisfaction for Himself. (3) In the repetition of this phrase, we see that God created the world in measured steps. That the elements of creation were arranged in order of increasing complexity on successive "days" suggests that God planned and designed the universe, creating it deliberately in an orderly fashion. He was like an artist who patiently worked, observed, and then continued working until everything was perfect. (4) In the repetition of this phrase, we see God demonstrating His dominion over everything in His creation by naming it. He knew what each thing was meant to be.

2. a. Genesis 1:2 tells us that "the Spirit" (lit. *ruah* in Hebrew, or "breath") was also present at creation.

b. The Spirit was "moving over the face of the waters," or hovering expectantly over the unformed chaos that was about to become the earth. This description suggests that God's Spirit was an integral part of all the action of creation.

105

3. The use of the plural "us" and "our" in Genesis 1:26 suggests two things about God. First, like the royal "we," it reflects His greatness, power, and majesty. The Hebrew plural noun used for God in the text, *Elohim,* suggests this as well. There, it is a plural of emphasis, not of number. In addition, there is also a longstanding Christian tradition of seeing in these plural pronouns an intimation of *communion,* or community, within the Godhead. They suggest that God, although One, is not solitary. This eventually was explicitly revealed in salvation history as the Blessed Trinity (see next question).

4. *Challenge question:* The New Testament reveals that *Jesus* was the "word" that God spoke "in the beginning." He was present as the creative Word of God. Jesus' role was to create and to sustain the universe and life: "[A]ll things were made through him" (Jn. 1:3); "in him all things were created . . . all things were created through him and for him. He is before all things, and in him all things hold together" (Col. 1:16–17). From the very first words of Scripture, we are introduced to the Word of God, who will, throughout all the rest of its pages, slowly but magnificently be revealed. He was fully manifested when He took on human flesh in the womb of Mary, becoming the Incarnate Son of God.

5. Responses will vary. As God thought, planned, executed, and evaluated, man in His image should be expected to do the same; in other words, man will be rational. God's boundless creativity was a central aspect of His creation. Surely, man will likewise be creative. All God created was good and well-ordered; even so we would expect man to have an appreciation of goodness and order. The care God exhibited for creation leads us to expect compassion and care in man. The eternal nature of God, living outside of time, suggests a capacity for eternal life in man. And the fact that God, although One, was not alone but existed in communion with the Word and the Spirit prepares us to expect a need for communion among men. They will not be solitary creatures.

6. God, who is Spirit, and thus neither male nor female, is nonetheless reflected in mankind by male and female together. Man and woman are created "equal as persons . . . and complementary as masculine and feminine" (*Catechism,* no. 372). Each has the inherent dignity of being created in God's image. In communion together, and particularly in the context of the family, they fully reflect the image of the Divine Family, which is God the Father, Son, and Holy Spirit.

7. *Challenge question:* All that God made pleased and satisfied Him. Everything was filled with goodness, since it all came from God Himself. To be blessed by God, in this context, was to be *pleasing in His sight.* Man and animal were in complete harmony with the purpose God had in creating them. This is an important idea to grasp at this moment in Genesis. As Catholic students of Scripture, we will want to keep a very close eye on what becomes of this blessing that God has given to man. The blessing of God—how we got it, how we lost it, and how we'll get it back (and keep it)—is the central focus of all salvation history. The entire Bible can be summed up as the story of this drama. Because of its importance in the rest of Scripture, linger here in Genesis 1 and soak in just how magnificent it was for man and beast to be blessed by God at the dawn of creation.

8. a. God's blessing of both man and animals included a charge to be fruitful and multiply and fill the earth. In addition, man was charged with subduing the earth and having dominion over it. *Dominion* means "supreme authority; sovereignty." God, who is absolute King over all His creation, shares His authority with man by entrusting him with the earth and its resources, thus giving man the dignity of cooperating with Him in completing the work of creation. Man's dominion is not intended to be domination; he is, rather, to care for the earth, to oversee it, to work it, and enjoy its fruits.

b. Man's work on earth was to be like God's work in creation. In giving man the responsibility to be fruitful, God allowed him to participate in the creation of human life. In giving him charge over the earth, God vested man with some of His own authority, asking man to share in His work of ruling. Man's two-part vocation was thus a reflection of God Himself. It enabled him to be what he was created to be—a creature made in God's image. And in fulfilling this vocation, he would find true happiness.

9. a. God gave them food to nourish and sustain them (vv. 29–30).
b. In this provision of food, God made it clear that He is the source of all that living creatures need for their lives to be sustained. It is of great importance for Catholics to recognize this simple provision from God, which appears so early in Genesis. In connecting Himself to the sources of food for man and beast, God showed Himself to be the true nourishment of all life. Is it any wonder, therefore, that the Church has, as its central act of worship of God, the provision of a heavenly meal for man, the Body and Blood of Christ?

10. Responses will vary. It is difficult to answer this from Genesis 1 alone. However, given God's self-sufficiency and limitless perfection, and having observed the great care with which God fashioned the earth for us, it is reasonable to assume we are here because He knew we would enjoy living and knowing Him. He created us for His good pleasure and our own. Theologian Frank J. Sheed has this to say: "It is a new light upon the love of God that our gain could be a motive for His action. He knew that beings were possible who could enjoy existence, and He gave them existence. By existing they glorify Him—but who is the gainer by that? Not God, who needs nothing from any creature. Only the creature, whose greatest glory is that He can glorify God."[1]

---

[1] Frank J. Sheed, *Theology for Beginners* (Ann Arbor, MI: Servant Books, 1981), 49.

Lesson 2

To make the most of this study, respond to all the questions yourself before reading these responses.

Completion and Rest: The Seventh Day (Gen. 2:1–3)

1. God rested not because He was tired, but because He was finished. Nothing formless or empty remained in the world; it was complete and perfect. In His essence, God is not just a being who works. He is a being who *is*—He exists complete in Himself. When God rested from His work, He was in glad harmony and communion with all His works. When God's creative work was finished, He gave man the task of continuing that creative work and caring for it. By resting on the seventh day He set a pattern, a rhythm of work and rest, that would one day be reproduced in man's life on earth—six days to work, and one day to enjoy and celebrate his glad harmony and communion with God.

The Creation of Man (Gen. 2:4–7)

2. a. God created man in His own image and after His likeness. Whereas He told the waters and the earth to bring forth creatures, God Himself formed man "from the dust from the ground, and breathed into his nostrils the breath of life."

b. This breath of life is the soul, "that by which (man) is most especially in God's image" (*Catechism*, no. 363). It is this that separates man from the animals. They are living beings, with the spirit of life in them, but they do not have this soul that comes from God. Breathed into him by God Himself, man's soul has free will and is incorruptible.

The Creation of the Garden (Gen. 2:8–17)

3. a. The Garden was full of trees that were "pleasant to the sight" and "good for food." There were two special trees in the midst of the Garden—one was the Tree of Life; the other was the Tree of Knowledge of Good and Evil.

b. The Garden was a place where man was fully alive and in complete harmony with the purposes for which God designed him. His senses, a gift to him from God, were able to take in the beauty of creation. As the *Catechism* says, "The beauty of creation reflects the infinite beauty of the Creator and ought to inspire the respect and submission of man's intellect and will" (no. 341). The Garden's beauty was to be a reminder to man of the goodness and wisdom of God.

c. *Challenge question:* The beauty of the Garden makes us expect beauty wherever God and man meet on earth. We are not surprised, then, when we find unutterable beauty in the place where God first met man outside the Garden, that is, in the worship of Israel. In the tabernacle, built by Moses when the Hebrews had escaped from Egypt, the holy of holies was the place where God and man, in the person of the high priest, met. It was a place of extraordinary beauty, since its walls were covered with gold. It contained the ark of the covenant, a box containing the tablets of stone on which the Ten Commandments were written. The ark was covered in gold and had exquisite heavenly sculptures on it (see

Ex. 25:10–22). The vestments of the high priest were studded with gems so that, when he went into the tabernacle on behalf of the people to do his priestly work, he was arrayed in "glory and beauty" (see Ex. 28:40). The Catholic Church's tradition of exquisite beauty in her architecture and art continues what we see here in Genesis. God intends for man to experience beauty in His presence. As Saint Thomas Aquinas taught, man's senses are ordered to beauty.[2] (See also *Catechism,* nos. 2502–3.)

4. Responses will vary. The need to keep or "guard" the Garden makes one ask, "against what?" After all, this is Paradise, is it not? And haven't we just seen that God called all creation "very good?" This is a curious detail at this point in the story, one we will want to keep in mind.

5. *Challenge question:* It is clear in this scene that God designed man with the capacity to make a choice that would determine his fate. Man understood that the choice to disobey God would result in death. Long before the serpent tempted him, he was aware of good and evil. "Good" meant living the way God asked him to, and living forever; "evil" meant disobeying God and facing death. We can see that man was, at the beginning, designed to achieve the end for which he was created by means of a choice. Of course, it had to be a *real* choice (what kind of choice would it have been if God had told man not to eat the thorns from a misshapen bush?). Because God is Himself free, He desires man to freely choose to love and obey Him. The choice was man's to make.

The Creation of Eve (Gen. 2:18–25)

6. a. Being alone is not good because God is not alone. Within the one God are three distinct, equal Persons in a communion of love. Man alone, without an equal, could not be fully in God's image. Man must be in communion with others like himself, in order to be all that God created him to be. In that communion, he reflects the Blessed Trinity.

b. Because the creation was an active work of all three Persons of the Trinity, man needed one who could help him do his work of fruitfulness and dominion—"a helper fit for him." A "companion" is one who keeps another company; a "helper" shares his work.

7. Adam's not finding a suitable helper among the animals was for his own benefit. He knew from his own experience that, while he was like the beasts of the field in many ways, he was different and set apart from them. He needed his helper to be one equal to himself. Notice here that this kind of knowledge is something Adam reached through his own experience. It was different from the knowledge that was revealed to him by God. God told him what to eat and what not to eat in the garden. It wasn't left up to him. Man's knowledge in the Garden was of two types: one was revealed knowledge, and the other was knowledge obtained through experience and reason.

---

[2] Saint Thomas Aquinas, *Summa Theologica* I, q. 91, art. 3, rep. obj. 3.

8. Responses will vary. God went into the body of Adam to create a creature truly equal to him, yet different from him. Man and woman were remarkably similar, but they were not exactly the same. By creating the second human being on earth in this way, God guaranteed equality among human beings, in spite of their differences.

9. **a.** Adam recognized that Eve, as one like him, could really be his helper, unlike the animals. Adam's work on earth was to be fruitful and have dominion over the earth. He needed someone who could work in the same way he did (with reason, hands, etc.) He also needed someone with whom he could produce offspring. If he looked at Eve's body and his own, he would have seen that they "fit," that they were meant to go together. She was just what he was looking for!

b. In the context of verses 23–24, marriage is the happy union of man and woman that enables each to be what God intended for human beings. Their marriage means that they are not alone. It also means that they can fulfill their work of fruitfulness and dominion. They can be fruitful because their "cleaving" will produce the "one flesh" both of intimacy *and* of offspring. They can have dominion because they will help each other with the work of maintaining what God created. In Genesis 2, marriage appears as the culmination of God's creative work—a source of joy to both the humans and to Himself.

c. "One flesh" is both the sign and the expression of the indissoluble union of marriage. When a man and a woman come together in marriage, they become, in effect, a new, indivisible creation. The child that their cleaving begets is the expression of that oneness. As the Catholic marriage rite says, "You gave man the constant help of woman so that man and woman should no longer be two, but one flesh, and you teach us that what you have united may never be divided." This is simply a statement of what Jesus teaches in the Gospels. Marriage was always intended by God to be permanent.

10. *Challenge question:* Genesis 2 helps us to see the full purpose of conjugal union in marriage. It has a divine dynamic, both for the production of new human life *and* for the fulfillment of husband and wife in their human vocation. Sexual union, with its intimacy and its power to keep creating human beings, was a great gift to Adam and Eve. We can see this clearly in Genesis 2. Preventing sexual union from accomplishing the purpose for which it was given distorts it and thus robs the creatures of its intended end. Understanding the clear picture here helps us to see that the teaching of the Church on "openness to life" and opposition to artificial contraception has preserved the truths of Paradise faithfully:

> Thus the innate language that expresses the total reciprocal self-giving of husband and wife is overlaid, through contraception, by an objectively contradictory language, namely, that of not giving oneself totally to the other. This leads not only to a positive refusal to be open to life but also to a falsification of the inner truth of conjugal love, which is called upon to give itself in personal totality. . . . The difference, both anthropological and moral, between contraception and recourse to the rhythm of the cycle . . . involves in the final analysis two irreconcilable concepts of the human person and of human sexuality. (*Catechism*, no. 2370, quoting *Familiaris Consortio* 32)

Lesson 3

To make the most of this study, respond to all the questions yourself before reading these responses.

The Challenge (Gen. 3:1–3)

1. The serpent was "that ancient serpent, who is called the Devil and Satan, the deceiver of the whole world." In the heavenly vision from Revelation, he is described as a great red dragon, with seven crowned heads and ten horns. The crowns and horns represent his tremendous power—he is a creature that strikes fear and dread into the souls of mere men. The *Catechism* helps us to understand that Satan was once a good angel who "radically and irrevocably rejected God and His reign" (no. 392). In addition to being a rebel against God's authority, he is "a liar and the father of lies" (Jn. 8:44). He was an enemy of God's first human creatures, seducing them to fall into disobedience and death. He even tried to "divert Jesus from the mission He received from the Father" (*Catechism*, no. 394). Although he is clearly powerful and intimidating, Satan is still a *creature* in God's universe. His power to wreak havoc is finite. This truth will become abundantly clear as we move through the rest of Genesis 3.

2. a. We have to wonder why God would allow His enemy to enter the sanctuary of the Garden and tempt His creatures to disobedience.

b. *Challenge question:* As surprised as we are by the appearance of the serpent, we realize the serpent could never have gotten into the Garden without God's permission. In the first chapter of Genesis, we saw that God created all things. There cannot be any creature with a power equal to or independent of Him. Even though the serpent is clearly evil, he did not get into the Garden by some horrible cosmic accident. If we took seriously the rich details of God's goodness in the first two chapters, we must conclude that, however it may appear to us, His goodness was not violated in this episode. There is no other reasonable conclusion, although it is not one easy to embrace. "To this question [why does evil exist?], as pressing as it is unavoidable and as painful as it is mysterious, no quick answer will suffice" (*Catechism*, no. 309). The irrefutable testimony of Genesis 1–2 to God's character helps us to have hope, in spite of appearances. "We firmly believe that God is master of the world and of its history. But the ways of his providence are often unknown to us. Only at the end, when our partial knowledge ceases, when we see God 'face to face,' [1 Cor. 13:12] will we fully know the ways by which—even through the dramas of evil and sin—God has guided his creation to that divine Sabbath rest [cf. Gen. 2:2] for which he created heaven and earth" (*Catechism*, no. 314).

3. a. Responses will vary. We know from the *Catechism* that Satan rebelled against God's authority. If Adam had been given a charge by God to guard the Garden, he was God's appointed representative there. The serpent bypassed him completely. His pitch, addressed to the woman, was an act of insubordination, perfectly in keeping with his character.

The serpent may have also recognized the importance of the woman's vocation as mother. In reflecting on the "Proto-evangelium" in Genesis, Pope John Paul says, "The 'woman', as mother and first teacher of the human being (education being the spiritual dimension of parenthood), has a specific precedence over the man. Although motherhood, especially in the bio-physical sense, depends upon the man, it places an essential "mark" on the whole personal growth process of new children. . . . [M]otherhood *in its personal-ethical sense* expresses a very important creativity on the part of the woman, upon whom the very humanity of the new human being mainly depends."[3]

b. Responses will vary. We can presume that Adam was right there with the woman as the serpent began his conversation. Why? In the Hebrew text of these verses, all the verbs the serpent used were in the second person plural. His references were to *both* the man and the woman, although his attention was directed towards the woman. In verse 6, we know that the woman gave some of the forbidden fruit to her husband. In order to translate the Hebrew more accurately than our RSV text does, one Bible renders this as "she gave some to her husband, who was there with her" (the New International Version or NIV Bible). That is the more literal sense of the verse.

4. a. God said to Adam, "[Y]ou *may freely eat* of every tree of the garden." The serpent changed the command from a positive ("you may freely eat . . . except one") to a negative ("you shall not of every tree"). That changed the command from being essentially an invitation to being essentially a prohibition. The meaning, strictly speaking, was the same: either way, there was a tree that was forbidden. By emphasizing the one tree over the many, the serpent made the woman focus on what she couldn't have rather than on the bounty God provided for them.

b. The serpent's language implied that God was harsh and restrictive, when actually He wanted His creatures to live freely and be happy. With just a simple rephrasing of the command, a deceptive shadow was cast over God's character.

5. Responses will vary. It seems clear that the woman understood that eating from the tree was full of danger. Perhaps in her mind, she had resolved never to even touch that tree, since it had such a severe warning attached to it. She seems to have been making a noble effort to avoid contact with it at all costs.

The Deception (Gen. 3:4–5)
6. a. Everything the serpent suggested would happen as a result of eating the fruit was already possessed by the man and woman. Let's take a look:

"You will not die." It was true already that the humans were intended for immortality, because they were made in the image and likeness of God, who is

---

[3] Pope John Paul II, On the Dignity and Vocation of Women *Mulieris Dignitatis* (August 15, 1988), no. 19.

immortal. As we will discover later in Genesis 3, the fruit of the Tree of Life, which had been theirs for the taking, bestowed *eternal* life.

"Your eyes will be opened." Their eyes were already open. Adam saw the woman God presented to him and burst into exclamations of delight at the sight of her. Genesis 2:25 tells us that the man and the woman saw each other's nakedness without shame. There was nothing lacking in their eyesight.

"You will be like God." They were already like God in the greatest way possible for created beings. They were made in His image and likeness, a fact verified by the work He had given them of procreating and sustaining life on earth.

"Knowing good and evil." They already knew what God had revealed to them to be good and evil, although they had not yet experienced it. They knew that obedience to God's command was good, because it would preserve their lives with Him; they knew that disobedience was evil, because it would cause their death.

b. Responses will vary. The serpent suggested that God's prohibition against the fruit was for *His* sake, not for theirs. He implied that God did not want competition from the human creatures, so He prevented them from eating the fruit that would make them "like gods."

c. *Challenge question:* The serpent wanted the man and woman to break free from God's authority, implying that He couldn't be trusted to put the creatures' well-being first. He urged them to be independent and autonomous. Implicit in this temptation was a taunt: "Don't be such *creatures*. Have you no *pride*? Think for yourselves." How ironic that he urged them to grasp through rebellion what they already possessed through obedience.

A word from John Paul II is helpful here: "With this imagery, Revelation teaches that *the power to decide what is good and what is evil does not belong to man, but to God alone.* The man is certainly free, inasmuch as he can understand and accept God's commands. And he possesses an extremely far-reaching freedom, since he can eat 'of every tree of the garden.' But his freedom is not unlimited: it must halt before the 'tree of the knowledge of good and evil,' for it is called to accept the moral law given by God. In fact, human freedom finds it authentic and complete fulfillment precisely in the acceptance of that law. God, who alone is good, knows perfectly what is good for man, and by virtue of his very love proposes this good to man in the commandments."[4]

7. a. Responses will vary. Adam's status as child of God, husband of the woman, and keeper of the Garden required him to stand up in some way to the serpent. He should have stepped in to defend his bride, the Garden, and God's name in whatever way that battle had to be fought. If the thought of that was frightening to him, he could have cried out for help from God: "Oh, Father! What do I do now?" He should have given himself entirely to preserving the life God had given to him and the woman in the Garden.

---

[4] Pope John Paul II, Encyclical Letter *Veritatis Splendor* (August 6, 1993), no. 35

b. Responses will vary. It is impossible to know exactly why Adam was silent and passive in the Garden. Did the appearance of the serpent, who seemed to have superior knowledge to his own, intimidate him? Did it cause him to doubt God's trustworthiness? Was he silent because he was calculating the cost of opposing the serpent? Did he think it might cost him his life, or, if not his life, at least some pain? At the most basic level, the serpent's challenge caused Adam to wonder whether he could trust God. And uncertainty—as it does to us so often— rendered him speechless and unwilling to act. The *Catechism* says that "Man, tempted by the devil, let his trust in his Creator die in his heart, and, abusing his freedom, disobeyed God's command. This is what man's first sin consisted of [see Gen. 3:1–11; cf. Rom. 5:19]. All subsequent sin would be disobedience toward God and lack of trust in His goodness. In that sin man *preferred* himself to God and by that very act scorned him. He chose himself over and against God, against the requirements of his creaturely status and therefore against his own good" (nos. 397–98). Adam's silence in the Garden was the sound of death.

c. Adam's unwillingness to act left the woman vulnerable to the serpent. She was left to manage all on her own. She had valiantly tried to ward off the serpent's earlier suggestion to reconsider God's prohibition against eating the forbidden fruit, but what effect did Adam's silence and inaction have on her? Adam's self-donation to the cause of opposing the serpent would have confirmed her in what she knew to be true about God. His living example of putting complete trust in God's word could have led her to do the same. Instead, she was the only one in the Garden who had not capitulated to rebellion against God. She was all alone, and it is never good for man to be "alone."

The Decision (Gen. 3:6)

8. a. The tree was pleasing to the sight, a delight to the senses. The fruit looked tasty. Even the name of the tree—the tree of knowledge—sounded appealing. Everything about the tree—its look, its feel, its effects—seemed irresistibly desirable.

b. The beauty and desirability of the tree *should* have served to remind the woman of the goodness of God. The tree ought to have been a physical representation of the care, wisdom, and love of God. God wasn't standing there in the Garden, rehearsing how He had done everything necessary to provide for His children. The goodness of creation was His silent witness. But once this focus was lost, the woman lost her way.

c. *Challenge question:* When the woman saw *only* the tree before her, she set all her affection on it. Forgetting God, she loved what He had created more than she loved Him. Saint John tells us in 1 John 2:15–17 that love of (inordinate attachment to) the world or the things of the world cannot coexist with love for the Father. The world is not an end in itself. Its splendor is meant to lead us to God and to make us want to live in obedience to its Creator. If our focus shifts from God, who created the world, to the world He created, we lose our way as the woman did. That is why Saint John tells us that love of the world short-circuits our lives. Our affection is meant only for God, and because of Him, for other people. The world is much too small and temporal to bear it. Like an overloaded fuse, if our love rests on the world, our lives are snuffed out; only "he who does the will of God abides for ever."

9. a. Sometimes we're inclined to think this test wasn't fair because of its severity. It is important for us to guard against this reaction. We need to recall what the man and woman knew about God and about themselves before the appearance of the serpent. It might help if we make a list:

- They knew that they existed through the will and power of God.
- They knew that this God was good and cared for every aspect of their lives.
- They knew that even their communion with each other was literally a gift from God's hand.
- They knew that they were like God because they could procreate and have dominion over the earth.
- They knew that God had revealed to them what was good (obedience) and what was evil (disobedience).
- They knew death existed as a consequence of disobedience.

Once we conclude that the man and woman knew enough to pass the test, we wonder why they didn't. That will be our next question.

b. The man and woman should have been able to trust the goodness of the invisible God, no matter what appeared before them. The visible goodness of Eden testified loudly to God's character. Although Adam was not able to "see" God, his own knowledge and experience of God's goodness should have enabled him to have the courage to repel the enemy from the Garden, no matter what the cost. In other words, the man and woman should have exercised *faith*, which is trust in God, who cannot be seen. Faith believes that God exists, and faith expresses that belief in obedience to the unseen God.

Lesson 4

To make the most of this study, respond to all the questions yourself before reading these responses.

Discovery and Effect (Gen. 3:7–13)

1. a. The eyes of Adam and Eve were opened to see the world *without* the "grace of original holiness" (*Catechism*, no. 399). The world they perceived had not changed, but the *way* they perceived it had been radically altered. The supernatural grace that God had given them died through their disobedience. That grace had been the lens through which they perceived and experienced reality. The serpent's enticement had been a half-truth. Eating the fruit did open their eyes, but that opening brought blindness, not sight.

Christopher West helps us to understand how these "opened" eyes worked:

Adam and Eve no longer clearly saw in each other's bodies the revelation of God's plan of love. They each now saw the other's body more as a thing to use for their own selfish desires. In this way the experience of nakedness in the presence of the other—and in the presence of God—became an experience of fear, alienation, shame: 'I was afraid, because I was naked, and I hid myself' (Gen. 3:10).

Their shame was connected not so much with the body itself but with the lust now in their hearts. For they still knew that since they were created as persons for their own sakes, they were never meant to be looked upon as things for another person's use. So they covered their bodies to protect their own dignity from the other's lustful "look." This is, in fact, a positive function of shame, because it actually serves to protect "nuptial meaning of the body."[5]

No wonder Jesus told His disciples, "The eye is the lamp of the body. So, if your eye is sound, your whole body will be full of light; but if your eye is not sound, your whole body will be full of darkness. If, then, the light in you is darkness, how great is the darkness!" (Mt. 6:22–23).

b. Adam and Eve could no longer face their Creator and Father openly. They hid from Him among the trees. Had God changed? No, He was the same God, but their disobedience filled them with fear, making them want to flee from communion with Him in the Garden.

2. **a.** Responses will vary. God knew everything that had happened, but He asked them for an accounting of their behavior because He wanted them to put into words what they had done. He did this for their sakes, not His. It would have allowed them to have enough self-knowledge to recognize how far they had departed from the life God had designed for them.

b. *Challenge question:* By asking Adam and Eve for an explanation of their rebellion, God acknowledged that who they were and why they did what they did was important to him. God was the good Father in the Garden. His primary concern was for *them*. Their words mattered to Him. He gave them an opportunity to take responsibility for their actions and cast themselves on His mercy. This interrogation was meant to lead to restoration, an incredible sign of hope.

3. **a.** Adam blamed his disobedience on Eve, and, indirectly, on God, since He was the One who had given her to Adam. This response represented a dramatic change from Adam's perception of Eve before the Fall (Gen. 2:23). There he had been able to see her for who she really was—a gift from God's hands, to fulfill his life on earth. After the Fall, Adam saw her as the cause of all his problems. The man who had been put in charge of the Garden denied any culpability for its violation.

---

[5] West, *Good News About Sex and Marriage*, 23–24.

b. Eve likewise blamed the serpent, who had beguiled her.

4. Adam and Eve did not take personal responsibility for their actions. There was no evidence of remorse or grief over their disobedience—no crying out for forgiveness. With their new eyesight, they could not see how offensive their behavior was to their Father. It wasn't that they were unaware of what they had done. They were unaware of what it meant.

5. a. *Challenge question:* As a direct result of their disobedience, Adam and Eve saw everything in their world differently. First, they saw themselves as naked, which caused shame. Second, they saw God as One to fear and avoid at all costs. Third, they lost sight of each other as helpers and companions. They were fearful and defensive. Although their bodies were alive, something inside of them had died. It was an interior death, affecting every aspect of their lives; it was the death of grace in their souls.

b. Responses will vary. Perhaps the most devastating consequence of their disobedience was that the new eyesight promised by the serpent had left them unable to see what they had become. There was no repentance, no remorse over their break with God. When God asked Adam, "Where are you?" Adam explained that he didn't want to be seen by God in his nakedness. The center of his concern was *himself.* "*I* heard the sound . . . *I* was afraid . . . *I* was naked . . . *I* hid myself" (v. 10). How far he had come from his original relationship with God! Yet there is no evidence from the text that he and Eve knew that they were spiritually dead. There was only self-preservation and defensiveness. How great was the darkness.

Curse and Promise (Gen. 3:14–15)
6. Satan was the actual villain here. He was God's true enemy. This is not to deny the humans' responsibility, but the first order of business was to address this one who seemed to have gained such power over them. They would not be safe as long as he could wield that power.

7. By God's curse, the serpent was destined to be the most wretched creature on earth—cursed "above all cattle" and "all wild animals." He would be the lowest form of life, a status that would be evident even in how he moved from place to place ("upon your belly"), eating dust. The meaning was clear: Satan had gone from his position of pride and power to one of lowliness and impotence. His demise was lightening-quick. This sudden and irrevocable fall of Satan is a common theme in Scripture, as the other readings make clear.

8. a. Yes, a battle already existed in the rebellion of Satan against God.

b. God's announcement meant that He was going to extend the battle to include the human beings. Initially, the humans had been targets of the devil's wrath against God. But now God would enlist the humans on His side. Could the serpent have possibly imagined this incredible twist? It is the first great reversal in the story of man. From this point on, *reversal* will be the underlying theme of our human history. Pause now to think carefully about this. However we come to understand ourselves and our world, we must get this one truth firmly in place—God does His work through *reversals*.

9. The serpent had aimed his attack at Eve. It was through her act of disobedience that the first bite was taken. It was therefore appropriate that God's punishment on the serpent should begin with "the woman." Whatever had been lost from woman's dignity as a creature in God's image would be restored by the "woman" of the battle God announced.

10. a. The "woman" and "her seed" would work *against* God's enemy, not for him, as Adam and Eve had done through their disobedience. They would stand outside of his power and authority, working as co-laborers with God, as Adam and Eve had originally been destined to do.

b. The question this phrasing provokes is: Why was there no husband mentioned in this scenario? The only "he" is the seed of the woman, not her mate. How can a woman have a child without a husband?

11. a. A head wound suggests one that completely incapacitates. What else does a serpent have to keep him in action beside his head? A bruise on the heel, although painful and aggravating, is not one that would end the life of a man.

b. The outcome of this battle will mean the defeat of God's enemy, although it will not come without pain to "the seed."

c. Responses will vary. Remember the contempt for the humans that filled the serpent when he began that deadly conversation that he had with Eve. The devil despised Adam and Eve. They must have looked like such dupes to him. He decided he would strike out at God by striking out at them, since they appeared to be weak links in the chain. He made patsies of them in short order. So, when God announced that, as his punishment, the serpent would face a battle with human creatures (the woman and her seed) in which he would be defeated, it was a crushing, mortal blow to his pride and arrogance. We need to linger long enough to let it really sink in. Whatever the devil attempted to rob from humanity—our life, our dignity, our exalted position in God's family—was more than made up for in the punishment meted out to him. God will vanquish His enemy *through* human beings!

d. The promise of God to defeat His enemy through human beings, creatures who had just betrayed Him in the Garden, was a promise so full of hope that it swells and bursts into a vision of glory bright enough to make us want to shield our eyes from it. Who *is* this God, who loves His creatures so much that He would allow them to participate this way in His plan to defeat evil? How could such faithless beings matter so much to Him? The details we have in the story thus far hardly explain it. We are forced to recognize that behind the words and actions we see in Genesis is an unseen love that is fathomless, mysterious, unconquerable, and capable of unimaginable displays of power and constancy. In the middle of the worst thing that could possibly have happened, hope trumped everything.

Lesson 5

To make the most of this study, respond to all the questions yourself before reading these responses.

Disobedience Punished (Gen. 3:16–19)

1. a. Responses will vary. Good parents punish their children out of love for them. If they find behavior in a child that will put him in immediate or long-term physical or moral danger, they introduce a measure of suffering (in the form of punishment) in order to prevent the greater suffering that such behavior, left unchecked, will produce. Punishment has several purposes: (1) it reminds a child of his parents' authority over him and that he is not autonomous; (2) it teaches him that his actions have consequences; and (3) it aims to deter a recurrence of the wrong behavior.

b. *Challenge question:* Punishment is a paradoxical sign of hope. Although to the child it may appear as anger or even hatred in the parents, good parents use it for rehabilitation. They know their child is capable of something better. Their love wants the very best for him. They are willing to appear like ogres in their child's limited sight because they are confident that, despite appearances, they are working for that child's ultimate happiness and well-being. Good parents are willing to risk the temporary loss of affection from their child in order to do what is best for him. They always take the long view; their hope for something better never dies. The Hebrews passage assures us that God is a good Father, who treats us as His own sons when He disciplines us. His discipline has a purpose, just like that of human parents. It aims to enable us to share His holiness, even though, at the time, it seems painful. This is a truth we will want to hold onto as we make our way through this part of Genesis 3.

2. As a punishment for her sin, Eve would give birth to children in great pain. Nevertheless, she would desire to be married, even though her relationship with her husband would be radically altered. The equality and dignity of her role as his helpmate would be gone; instead, her husband would rule over her, which was a terrible distortion of God's design for marriage. (Think of the symbolic meaning of the fact that after the Fall, all human beings entered the world through pain. What a graphic, unmistakable clue that mankind is under a curse, that things are not as they should be.)

3. a. Adam had delighted in the creation of Eve because she was his equal. She was to be the remedy for his loneliness; she was given to him to assist him in his work on earth. Because she came from him and was made for him, he would exercise a role of authority in their relationship. As Saint Paul says, "For man was not made from woman, but woman from man. Neither was man created for woman but woman for man" (1 Cor. 11:8–9). Their relationship was to be characterized by joy, harmony, cooperation, and mutual satisfaction, as the two became "one flesh" in marriage. But the effect of sin would be to shatter all this. Adam's "guardianship" of his wife as husband would become "rule." Adam would be tempted to tyranny and domination, a radical departure from the image and likeness of God in him. That would leave him at odds with himself, which always causes anguish. Eve, as a result, would seem more like Adam's slave than his helpmate. For both, marriage would fall far short of its original ecstasy.

b. *Challenge question:* Saint Paul restored the "headship" of a husband to God's original design for it. In verse 21, he wrote, "Be subject to one another out of reverence for Christ." In those words, he reminds married people that their relationship is to be one of mutual self-donation. The husband is to give himself over entirely to the well-being of his wife; the wife is to give herself over entirely to the well-being of her husband. This is the essence of the love of the Trinity, made manifest on the Cross, when Christ emptied Himself, even unto death, for the sake of sinners. We remember that in the Garden, Adam refused to accept responsibility for his wife's safety. He did not act as her "head." By his inaction, he capitulated to the serpent, which led to Eve's disobedience. The curse of sin on marriage meant that Adam moved from one extreme to the other—from passivity to domination, both of which are rooted in self-love, not self-donation. Saint Paul says that Christian husbands are to love their wives as they love their own bodies (vv. 28–29). That is a restoration of Adam's exclamation in the Garden: "This at last is bone of my bone and flesh of my flesh!" The headship of Christian husbands is to protect and nurture their wives. Paradoxically, a husband is "subject" to his wife by his willingness to take responsibility for her. Likewise, a wife is "subject" to her husband by her willingness to respect her husband's decisions about how he can best love her. (For further reflection on this passage, see "Marriage: Sacrament of Christ and the Church," p. 42).

c. As a punishment for listening to his wife instead of to God, Adam's work of dominion over the earth, to subdue it, would turn to toil. The ground was cursed so that it would resist cultivation. His daily work would be full of the sweat of frustration, aggravation, and futility.

4. *Challenge question:* Responses will vary. Recall that the most frightening consequence of the death of grace in Adam and Eve's lives was the distortion and disordering of their spiritual and physical faculties. They ran and hid from God; they wanted to remain autonomous from Him and from each other. How would God break through this wall of pride and darkness? How would He convince His children that their happiness was in His hands? Because their choice to turn to Him had to be a free one, He gave them reasons to make that choice. And so pain and suffering entered the human story. If, in their pride and fear of God, they would not run into His arms, would pain and suffering drive them to Him? They did not lose their knowledge that God exists when they disobeyed. But they could not see Him for who He is. If their lives became an experience of weakness, trouble, and desperation, would they humbly cry out for their Father's help? This kind of additional punishment of

Adam and Eve was meant to help them do the best possible thing—cast themselves on God for His mercy and help. If it had to come through pain and suffering, so be it. Better to experience short-term pain than to endure the everlasting pain and darkness of separation from God.

5. When God announced that man would return to dust, without the breath of God to animate him, He made clear the scope of what was lost in the Garden. The Church teaches us that "Even though man's nature is mortal, God had destined him not to die. Death was therefore contrary to the plans of God the Creator and entered the world as a consequence of sin [cf. Wis. 2:23–24]" (*Catechism*, no. 1008). Man, designed to be immortal, would ever after dread death as unnatural and contrary to what he knows himself to be.

A Severe Mercy (Gen. 3:20–24)

6. **a.** Responses will vary. Once, Adam had named the animals; was he taking charge of his wife in that kind of way? Another possibility exists: perhaps he was taking charge because of his previous failure. Perhaps the words of God's rebuke for listening to the voice of his wife were still with him. This may be Adam's first attempt to do things the *right* way. It's an interesting point to ponder.

b. The name Adam gave his wife, Eve, was one that was full of hope. Perhaps he was overjoyed to know that not only would they continue to live but that "the woman" and "her seed" would figure prominently in God's battle with His enemy. Possibly, this exalted role of mother moved him to choose that name for her. There's an irony in it, of course. Eve would become the mother of the spiritually dead. It would take another woman to be Mother of all the spiritually living. But in the name Eve, there was hope.

It is interesting to note that the Fathers of the early Church frequently saw in this naming of Eve an identification of her as a "virgin" mother. They noted that the record of the consummation of Adam and Eve's marriage doesn't appear until *after* they had left the Garden (see Gen. 4:1). Therefore, Eve received her name as "mother of all living" while she was still a virgin in the Garden.

7. God cared about these people. The fig leaves would not provide the covering they needed—too insubstantial. He wanted them to be properly clothed, in garments that would last.

8. *Challenge question:* The first shedding of blood on earth happened when God acted to cover the shame of Adam and Eve. It was the first episode of innocence covering guilt. The animals had not been created by God to serve this purpose. In the context of the story, it was a grave indication of the seriousness of sin and the lengths to which God would go to rescue man from it. Some have wondered about the power this detail from the creation story had on all civilizations that followed from Adam and Eve. Would the killing of an innocent animal become a gesture of remembrance or thanksgiving to God from men after that? Would they have an

impulse to offer up an animal in order to reenact this provision from God to clothe the nakedness of His fallen children? Does it have some connection with the universal practice of animal sacrifice among ancient cultures? Certainly it was a foreshadowing of the sacrifice of the Lamb of God, who takes away the sin of the world and covers the shame of all human beings.

9. a. God did not want the humans to eat from the Tree of Life and "live for ever." Why not? Surely it was because of the condition into which they had fallen. To live forever in a state of spiritual blindness and disorder in their natures would literally be a fate worse than death.

b. It is provocative to examine why God expelled man and woman from the Garden instead of just doing away with it. The expulsion, as severe as it seems, was actually a sign of unimaginable hope. It was truly a severe mercy. It suggested that the original plan of God for His human children did not die with the death of grace in them. Could it be that in allowing the Garden to remain, guarded by an angel and a flaming sword, God intended to return His creatures there *someday* to the life they once had? That, of course, would require healing the systemic wound in their natures. How could they ever receive a renewed human nature? When they left the Garden, with its Tree of Life, their physical bodies would be subject to death and decay. What would make it possible for human beings to eat from the Tree of Life and live forever?

10. *Challenge question:* Responses will vary. The departure of Adam and Eve from the Garden was tragic, but it was not a completely hopeless picture because of all the signs of God's love we have seen in this chapter. They left Paradise for a valley of tears, but the signs of hope were everywhere:

(1) God *punished* them. The pain that Adam and Eve (and thus all mankind) would experience in the realms that mattered most to them was a sign that God wanted to join them in their everyday existence. It would be a powerful motivation for them to cry out for Him. His punishment was aimed at restoring in them what once they had by nature—the ability to see that He was the source and protector of all that was important to them. The misery that would permeate the world would make life in it incapable of satisfying man's innate longing for goodness, truth, and beauty. This was a merciful blessing from God, who knew that His children, disordered as they were, would not on their own realize that they couldn't be content without Him.

(2) God *provided* garments to cover them in their shame and nakedness. In this He demonstrated to them, in a way that they could see and feel, that He still loved them. Even in their spiritual blindness, this was a sign they simply could not misunderstand.

(3) God *promised* to defeat His enemy and theirs in a battle to be waged through human beings—"the woman" and "her seed." The loss of dignity, honor, and glory that humans suffered because they betrayed God was only temporary. God had not given up on flesh and blood.

(4) God *preserved* the Garden on earth, with the Tree of Life. This sanctified place of extraordinary blessing and joy was not lost forever. This raised a flicker of hope that if God expelled them because He didn't want them to live eternally in their fallen condition, He might let them back in if somehow their condition could change. Knowing that God chooses to work by means of reversal, did Adam and Eve take with them a hope that Paradise could be regained?

Lesson 6
To make the most of this study, respond to all the questions yourself before reading these responses.

The Annunciation (Lk. 1:26–38)
1. Recall that the problem in the Garden of Eden was the loss of grace in Adam and Eve through their disobedience. For us to read this greeting of an angel to a young girl should make our hearts race. No one else in Scripture is addressed this way. The last woman to be "full of grace" on earth was Eve, before the Fall. If we have been waiting for a woman to appear in human history who is free from the consequences of the devil's deception and who will be God's agent in a battle against him, we have found her. The Greek word used here (*kecharitomene*) "indicates that God has already 'graced' Mary previous to this point, making her a vessel who 'has been' and 'is now' filled with divine life."[6] It is actually more like a title than a description. Gabriel's greeting to Mary marked her out as the woman for whom the world had been waiting. For a fuller explanation of Mary's life "full of grace," see the *Catechism*, nos. 490–93.

2. **a.** The "puzzle" of Genesis 3:15 was solved by a great mystery. The Father of the "seed" would be God Himself. This would be a most unusual Son! As we stood in the Garden with Adam and Eve, would we ever have dreamed that someday that Word through which the universe was created would take on human flesh— *human flesh!*—to undo the work of God's enemy?

   b. Perhaps Joseph was overwhelmed by the thought of marrying a woman who was pregnant by the Holy Spirit. Could we blame him? He had to be encouraged by an angel in a dream not to be afraid to take Mary into his home. This just man was chosen to give his name and his fatherly protection and care to the Son of God and Mary. His was a unique role.

3. **a.** Eve looked at the tree and its fruit with disregard for God's word about it. The fruit had great appeal to her, so she reached out and grasped it. She ate it, and she gave it to Adam to eat.

---

[6] Scott Hahn and Curtis Mitch, *Ignatius Catholic Study Bible: Gospel of Luke* (San Francisco: Ignatius Press, 2001), 19.

b. After hearing the angel's announcement, Mary received into her life God's word, which produced fruit in her womb, Jesus.

c. *Challenge question:* Eve disregarded God's word and grasped for what she wanted for herself. Mary believed God's word and received what He wanted to give her. Eve's disobedience led to death; Mary's obedience led to life. This was a spectacular reversal. No one has described it more beautifully than Saint Irenaeus (c. AD 140/160–202), who was Bishop of Lyons:

> Even though Eve had Adam for a husband, she was still a virgin. . . . By disobeying, she became the cause of death for herself and for the whole human race. In the same way, Mary, though she also had a husband, was still a virgin, and by obeying, she became the cause of salvation for herself and for the whole human race. . . . The knot of Eve's disobedience was untied by Mary's obedience. What Eve bound through her unbelief, Mary loosed by her faith.[7]

The Visitation (Lk. 1:39–56)

4. a. In the description of the Visitation, we have a marvelous opportunity to experience firsthand the joy of Israel at the coming of the Messiah. See that Luke tells us that Elizabeth "was filled with the Holy Spirit." Her utterance had the power of prophecy. As she jubilantly blessed Mary and the Child in her womb, Elizabeth gave voice to what all creation would want to sing out with "a loud cry" at the coming of the "woman" and her "seed" promised so long ago. Even the babe in Elizabeth's womb, John the Baptist, leaped for joy upon the arrival of the Mother and Son.

b. *Challenge question:* Notice that Elizabeth, in pronouncing her blessing, did not separate the Child from His Mother. Her blessing was on both of them together (1:42); she expressed reverence for both of them when she humbly asked why she should be the glad recipient of a visit from "the mother of my Lord." It was *Mary's* voice that caused the child in Elizabeth's own womb to leap for joy when he heard it. The promise of God in Genesis 3:15 led us to expect a woman and her seed to turn the tide against His enemy, the serpent. Both Elizabeth and John recognized the fulfillment of that promise in Mary and Jesus. The Church continues to appreciate and honor Mary for her role in redemption.

5. a. As the *Catechism* points out, it was Elizabeth who first described the source of Mary's blessedness: "[B]lessed is she who believed that there would be a fulfillment of what was spoken to her from the Lord" (1:45). It was Mary's unwavering trust in God that evoked the first act of veneration of her by Elizabeth when she said, "[W]hy is it granted to me, that the mother of my Lord should come to me?" (1:43). Because Mary "perfectly embodies the obedience of faith" (*Catechism*, no. 148), she has been called "blessed" by all generations since then.

---

[7] *Adversus haereses,* as quoted in Luigi Gambero, *Mary and the Fathers of the Church*, 52.

b. *Challenge question:* We know from the example of Elizabeth, who was full of the Holy Spirit when she blessed Mary, that it cannot possibly be wrong to bless and venerate her. Indeed, Mary herself said that "all generations shall call me blessed." So we see in Luke 11:27–28 that Jesus did not rebuke the woman in the crowd for honoring His Mother. He simply established the reason that Mary was to be honored. She was the one who had given birth to Him because she heard God's Word and kept it. Jesus wanted her to be honored for her faithful obedience, not simply because she was His biological mother.

The Presentation in the Temple (Lk. 2:22–35)

6. Simeon prophesied that suffering lay ahead for both Jesus and Mary. The Child was destined to initiate the messianic age in Israel. He would be a source of division, because some Jews would believe Him to be the Messiah and others wouldn't. His life, His teachings, and His Crucifixion would require a response from every Jewish heart. Simeon made that clear in his words to Mary. In the unusual phrasing of verse 35, he describes a time in the life of this Child when a sword would pierce through Him, and Mary was to share this moment. We know from accounts of the Crucifixion that when Jesus hung on the Cross, soldiers pierced Him with a sword to see if He was dead (Jn. 19:34). Simeon's words suggested that, in some way, Mary would be there with Him, with her own soul pierced. She would not simply be an observer of her Son's life. As both Jesus and Mary shared God's blessing, they were both to share in suffering.

As the *Catechism* tells us, all followers of Christ are invited to "'take up [their] cross and follow [him]' [Mt. 16:24]," because Jesus "desires to associate [them] with his redeeming sacrifice. . . . This is achieved supremely in the case of his mother, who was associated more intimately than any other person in the mystery of his redemptive suffering" (no. 618). This is precisely what Simeon prophesied.

The Wedding at Cana (Jn. 2:1–11)

7. It was Mary who was first aware of the wine shortage at the wedding feast. She took the problem to Jesus for resolution. She expected Him to do something about it, which is why she said to the servants, "Do whatever he tells you" (2:5). The miracle Jesus performed in response to her request was the beginning of His public manifestation as the Messiah. Mary and Jesus collaborated in this work of turning water to wine, which preserved the happiness of the marriage feast in Cana.

The Church sees in this episode Mary's work of manifesting the glory of Jesus (cf. 2:11). This was a fulfillment of her own statement about herself as a soul that "magnified the Lord" (Lk. 1:46). Mary's collaboration with Jesus in this initiation of His public ministry, which eventually led to "the hour" of His Crucifixion, and thus His glory, was a stunning reversal of Eve's collaboration with Adam in the Garden of Eden. There, Eve gave the forbidden fruit to Adam to eat, a collaboration that led to disobedience and death. At Cana, Mary's work with Jesus was a collaboration that led to celebration and joy.

The Crucifixion (Jn. 19:25–27)

8. *Challenge question:* Adam, in naming his wife "Eve," understood that she would have a maternal relationship to all humans on earth. She would be "mother" to all human beings, since they would all trace their physical beginnings back to her. In the gift of Mary to John, Jesus desired to make her "mother" to those who, like John, were His faithful followers. Those who are truly "living," who have been born again in the waters of Baptism, also have Mary as "mother." Because our new life comes through Jesus, we all trace our spiritual beginnings back to her, the one in whom God became flesh. There is, at last, a "Mother of all living."

A Vision of Heaven (Rev. 12:1–17)

9. **a.** The child is Jesus, the "one who is to rule all the nations with a rod of iron" (12:5). Thus, there is a strong indication that the woman is Mary, since she is His mother, the one who gave birth to Him.

b. The woman is clothed with the elements in heaven created by God to give light. "Let there be lights in the firmament of the heavens" is what He said at the time of creation (Gen. 1:14). These elements were to "give light upon the earth, to rule over the day and over the night" (Gen. 1:17–18). They were the only other creations of God, besides man and woman, to which He gave dominion. For the woman to be clothed with these elements suggests an exalted position of dominion in heaven. She appears like a queen, with a crown of twelve stars.

This is an image of Mary, as Queen of Heaven, that the Church holds dear. Her crown of twelve stars may represent the twelve tribes of Israel. Jews would have recognized that by virtue of being the mother of the Messiah, who was Son of David and royal ruler of Israel, Mary would have been queen of Israel. In ancient Israel, the queen was not the king's wife but his mother (since kings often had many wives). In 1 Kings 2:19, King Solomon was approached by his mother, Bathsheba, on behalf of someone making a request of him. "And the king rose to meet her, and bowed down to her; then he sat on his throne, and had a seat brought for the king's mother; and she sat on his right." Jews had great respect for the queen mother.

c. The dragon tried to devour the child, which he was not able to do. The child was taken up to heaven, to sit at God's throne. The woman was left behind, but she was "nourished by God."

10. **a.** The dragon, who is identified as "that ancient serpent . . . the Devil," (v. 9) was thrown down by the victory of the blood of the Lamb, as well as by the testimony of all those who loved Him more than their own lives. This is a fulfillment of the promise of Genesis 3:15—the serpent "bruised" the heel of the "seed," making Him shed blood. By shedding that blood, the "seed" bruised the head of the serpent, destroying all his power.

b. The serpent directed his wrath against the woman and the rest of her offspring. The woman was given special protection from his enmity. The Church sees in this vision the biblical basis for her teaching about Mary's Immaculate Conception, her sinless life, and her Assumption into heaven. The devil was never able to touch Mary's life with sin or its consequences. She is the woman "nourished by God" in Revelation. The Church, "all those who keep the commandment of God and bear testimony to Jesus," are her offspring.

11. *Challenge question:* Responses will vary. The gift of Mary, given to us by Jesus, adds immeasurably to our lives. Because we have retained Mary in our vision of the Redemption won by Jesus, we have the grace of meditating on her example of faithful obedience to the Word of God. Her wholehearted surrender to God's plan for her, the energetic assistance she gave to Elizabeth, her awareness of people in need at Cana, her confidence that Jesus could solve the problem, her perseverance through the ordeal of the Crucifixion, and her triumph as the Queen of Heaven—all these shed light on the path that we must follow in our journey home to God. Her life, magnified through the liturgies in her honor and through devotions to her like the rosary, keep her alive in our mind's eye. In that, she is a constant treasure to us.

Beyond that, we have the joy of sharing a Mother with Jesus. Her prayers and advocacy for us are as beautiful as the Magnificat and as effective as her work in Cana. Our recourse to her as our Mother acknowledges and keeps alive the wish of the dying Jesus, as He gave her to Saint John. Scripture tells us that from that moment the disciple took her to be his own. He recognized the great gift of Mary.

Finally, we know that, as Mary's offspring, "who keep the commandments of God and the testimony of Jesus," we are objects of the devil's wrath. She has been completely victorious over him; she knows what the battle is like. We are able to fly to the Queen of Heaven when we feel the full force of the enemy's enmity against us. In this battle, we are never alone.

Thank You, Jesus, for the gift of Mary in the Catholic Church.

Lesson 7

To make the most of this study, respond to all the questions yourself before reading these responses.

Jesus and the Devil (Lk. 22:39–46)

1. a. In the first two temptations of Jesus in the desert, Satan challenged Him to renounce His human limitations and act like the Son of God that He was. He taunted Jesus with the same challenge he gave to the woman: throw off the yoke of creatureliness. In the third temptation, Satan tried to win Jesus' allegiance away from God for himself. In this, he was a usurper, just as he was in the Garden. His aim in both places was to set himself up as a rival authority to God.

b. Jesus did not rise to the bait of Satan's temptations; He did not try to prove Himself. He freely accepted the limitations placed on Him by being human. In each temptation, Jesus answered the devil by quoting God's Word and referring to His commands. He chose humility, which is dependence on God, instead of the pride of autonomy. "Then the devil left him, and behold, angels came and ministered to him" (Mt. 4:11).

c. Right from the outset, as Jesus and the disciples entered the Garden of Gethsemane, Jesus seemed to have temptation on His mind. He warned His friends to pray so that they could ward off temptation. He knelt down in prayer to face the difficult moment of freely accepting His capture and death. An angel appeared to strengthen Him, just as angels had ministered to Him after His desert ordeal. Although there is no mention of the devil here, these are powerful clues that Jesus experienced the full force of temptation to preserve His life rather than lose it in a brutal assault. It was the temptation to avoid suffering, a scene of intense anguish.

2. In Genesis 3, God told Adam that his face would be covered with the sweat of his toil as a punishment for his disobedience. Adam's dominion over the earth, meant to be a source of joy for him, would instead bring him suffering. That Jesus' "sweat became like great drops of blood" in His garden presents a vivid picture of His taking upon Himself the curse placed on Adam (Lk. 22:44). The first Adam's disobedience was punishable by suffering and death. Jesus, the Second Adam, in the agony of the Garden, began to experience it. The sentence pronounced so long ago was now being executed.

3. Remember the deafening silence in the Garden of Eden when the serpent began his cunning attack? As we watched Adam stand there, perhaps weighing in his mind whether the serpent spoke the truth, didn't we long for him to cry out for help? We felt that just one cry could have changed everything. In these verses, we see a picture of Jesus doing precisely what Adam didn't do. He was afraid, but His fear led Him to call down help from His Father. This is the test of love that Adam did not endure. Love has to be a real choice, which means that it must be tested. Love of God leads one to continue to trust Him and to seek His help in the midst of the most threatening circumstances. It is a conscious, willful choice to believe in God's goodness, no matter what appearances suggest. This anguished cry of Jesus filled His garden with the sound of faith. It was a cry that reached heaven, undoing the silence of the Garden of Eden.

"Here Is the Man!" (Jn. 19:1–11)

4. *Challenge question:* If you have a picture of this scene in your mind's eye, it ought to make you catch your breath. Jesus, having been scourged, stood there in a purple robe and crown of thorns (remember the meaning of thorns in Eden in Genesis 3:17–18). Pilate's grand introduction was meant as mockery. The angry crowd was full of contempt for Jesus. And yet, this was a man in whom the likeness of God had not been lost, and the image has not been distorted (*Catechism*, no. 705, 1701–2). This was *man* as God always intended him to be—perfectly obedient and faithful to the covenant, no matter what the cost. In this Gospel scene, Jesus was the only one with real human dignity. He was the New Adam, and Pilate's announcement of "Here is the man!" heralded the beginning of a new humanity.

5. Jesus understood that power on earth is not without limitation; it is not autonomous, even when it can preserve or destroy physical life. He had confidence in God, which enabled Him to face frightening threats with courage and serenity. He recognized that no matter how things looked, God's plan would not be thwarted. This is just

what we wished we had seen in Adam, when his silence suggested that he was intimidated by the serpent, perhaps believing him to be a source of power and truth that rivaled God.

An Opened Side (Jn. 19:31–37)

6. Pathologists would tell us that a wound like this one, in its place on the body of one who died as Jesus died, would actually produce both blood and water. The Church has always recognized in this detail of Christ's death a startlingly beautiful symbol of the birth of the Church. The water of Baptism initiates believers into union with Christ; the Blood of the Eucharist sustains them on their journey to God (*Catechism,* no. 1225). In Scripture, the Church is frequently described as "the Bride" of Christ. The Lord refers to Himself as "the Bridegroom" (Mk. 2:19), and heaven will be the marriage feast of the Lamb (see *Catechism,* no. 796). In Eden, as Adam slept, God opened his side to create Eve, his bride, a true helper for him and one with whom he would form a permanent union in body and spirit. As Jesus slept the sleep of death on the Cross, the wound in His side poured forth the signs of His Bride, the Church. Adam, tempted by the devil, did not protect his wife with his life, but "Christ loved the Church and gave Himself up for her, that He might sanctify her" (Eph. 5:25–26).

Jesus, the Gardener (Jn. 20:11–18)

7. *Challenge question:* Who was the very first gardener on earth? It was Adam, of course. God planted a garden for Adam and put him in charge of it. Adam, however, failed in his responsibilities. He did not keep that garden safe and had to be sent away from it. For Mary Magdalene to mistake Jesus as the gardener is a profound clue to us of what actually happened in this garden of Resurrection. He is, in fact, the "Gardener." He is the New Adam, who will not fail to keep His Father's vineyard safe and make it fruitful. All things have been made new.

Suffering and Death (Heb. 2:5–18)

8. *Challenge question:* Remember that Adam was tested in Eden to prove his love for God. In the presence of an intimidating enemy, would he choose God's way, no matter what? In giving into the temptation of the serpent, he avoided the suffering of self-denial, of losing his opportunity to be "as gods." Although God had warned him of the fatal consequences of disobedience, he chose to satisfy himself in the short term and avoid suffering. Jesus, as the New Adam, had to retrace the human steps leading up to the first Adam's capitulation. For Him, it came down to a choice to obey God and suffer a torturous death, or to avoid suffering by putting His own welfare first. We know that Jesus embraced His suffering. He entered fully and without reserve the step that would be the final and unequivocal proof of His love for God. This was the step man was originally designed to take. It was part of God's plan to perfect in man the selfless love shared by the Blessed Trinity. As the *Catechism* says, "Angels and men, as intelligent and free creatures, have to journey toward their ultimate destinies by their free choice and preferential love" (no. 311). It was entirely fitting that Jesus should reach that destination through suffering, demonstrating for all eternity that man has nothing to fear (or lose) in trusting and obeying God.

9. a. *Challenge question:* The devil does not have ultimate power of life and death. He is only a creature; God alone has that power. These verses suggest that the "power" the devil has in death is the fear that it produces in human nature. The fear of death keeps men in bondage to the devil. How? Think of the scene in the Garden of Gethsemane. The fear of death in Jesus had the potential to turn Him away from God's will. In Jesus, we are able to see that choosing God over ourselves can be painful. It is a kind of death to ourselves. In the case of Jesus, it eventually led to a physical death as well. Think of Adam in Eden. To resist the temptation of the devil would have required a death in Adam—if not physical, then surely a death to what he wanted to gain by eating the forbidden fruit. When men are afraid to die to themselves, the devil uses that fear to entice them away from God.

b. When Jesus died and rose again, He stripped the devil of his most potent weapon against man. If death could not hold Jesus, He is really the One with power over it. He was "bruised" in the process, but in a great reversal, the death of Jesus, in spite of the appearance of victory for the devil, turned the world upside down, and the serpent slithered away with a mortal wound (see *Catechism*, no. 635). Men need only look at the Cross to know that obedience to God means victory over death. In losing our lives, we find them. We can see through the devil's sham.

A Surprising Solution (Jn. 3:1–15)

10. Jesus told Nicodemus that no one will see the kingdom of God without being "born anew." This comment addressed the radical problem man developed in Eden. How would he ever be able to enter the Garden and eat of the Tree of Life again unless he was healed of his debilitating condition of sin, which is lodged in his body and is passed along to his descendants? Jesus said it would take another birth, one of "water and the Spirit." This baffled Nicodemus, because it seemed so impossible and contrary to nature. Jesus registered surprise that Nicodemus, "a teacher of Israel," didn't understand this need for men to have a second birth. Yet we should understand it, because of what we know from Genesis. In fact, we longed for it when we watched Adam and Eve leave Paradise, but we couldn't imagine then how it would ever be possible. Now we know. Jesus announced to Israel, represented in the person of Nicodemus, that the victory He would win on the Cross ("the Son of Man must be lifted up") would be for anyone who believes in Him. The birth of "water and Spirit" is Baptism (read Rom. 6:1–11), the sacrament through which a believer is united to the death that Jesus died to sin and to the Resurrection which gives new life. The New Adam and Eve won't be alone in Paradise; all who believe in Jesus will join them through Baptism.

Eat and Live Forever (Jn. 6:47–59)

11. We know that the first "sacrament" appeared in Eden, where men could have eaten fruit and lived forever. Remember that Adam and Eve had to be sent out of Eden so they wouldn't eat from the Tree of Life and live forever in their fallen condition. For Jesus to offer Himself as food and drink for those seeking eternal life was a wonderful sign that the time had arrived for men to once again eat food for immortality. The Tree of Life was a prominent feature of life in Eden. Jesus told the Jews that "the bread which I shall give for the life of the world is my flesh" (v. 51). Thus, we understand that the "tree" of the Cross (see Acts 5:30), which is where Jesus gave His flesh, has born fruit for eternal life. In the Eucharist, we eat that "fruit" and live forever.

12. *Challenge question:* Responses will vary.

Holy water at all the entrances—the Garden was well-watered by a river that flowed out of it, dividing into four rivers. The water in church is a reminder that only by being born of water and the Spirit can man reenter Eden.

Beauty—Catholic churches are often beautiful, some dazzlingly so (think of Saint Peter's in Rome). In their beauty, they reproduce the great sensual beauty of Eden. Beauty is God's gift to man fully alive. It is His testimony to our senses that He exists; beauty reminds us that God, who created it, is worthy to be adored.

Sanctified time and space—In the beginning, God hallowed one day out of all the others for Himself. The Church continues to hallow time, identifiable through the liturgical colors of the altar cloths and vestments of the priests. Eden was sanctified space, a place set apart from the rest of the earth for God and man to meet in a unique way. The red tabernacle light alerts us to the continued reality of sanctified space. The Lord is present in the consecrated hosts; the ground of the church is holy ground.

Artistic representations of Jesus and Mary—A man and a woman presided over the first Garden, male and female in the image of God. A woman and her Son were promised to fallen humanity to begin the restoration of life in Eden. To see Jesus and Mary represented in a church, in statuary or art, should plant us deeply into the soil of joy. God has kept His promise to His creatures—the devil has been defeated through the New Adam and the New Eve. The stunning victory of God is complete!

Artistic representations of the saints—Adam and Eve were meant to begin a family, but the fall into disobedience intervened. The people who would have filled the Garden were born outside of it and not allowed in. In the Church, the saints represent the family of the New Adam and Eve. In Eden, Adam would have been the father of all who came after him. In the New Eden, God is the Father of Jesus and all who are "born anew." This means that Adam's fall resulted in a better life for us than would have been possible had he not fallen. Adam would have made us creaturely sons of God; Jesus makes us divine sons. The saints represented in churches remind us that God's family plan for Eden was not only preserved but elevated through the Redemption by Jesus. The human faces of the saints, upon which we gaze in church, give us more occasions to rejoice over God's triumphant humiliation of the serpent, who so loathed the creatures made of dust.

Crucifix—The Tree of Life in Eden offered fruit that was to be eaten for eternal life; the "tree" of the Cross offers fruit to be eaten for eternal life; it has become the Tree of Life.

Altar/Table—In Eden, God provided food for Adam and Eve to eat; in the New Eden, Christ welcomes us to share a meal of supernatural food and drink. In Eden, an innocent animal was sacrificed to provide covering for Adam and Eve. In the New Eden, the altar reminds us that an innocent man made an offering of His life to cover the guilty. The meal He offers is not a picnic meal. It is a sacrificial meal, which represents life in Eden both before and after the Fall, a meal that makes communion with God possible for helpless, redeemed sinners.

Confessionals—In Eden, God called Adam and Eve to give an account of their disobedience. They were free, and thus responsible for their actions. They showed no remorse for their sin. In the New Eden, men still have the freedom to choose to remain in God's covenant through obedience. If they fall, they can express their remorse and their resolve not to sin again in confession. They are restored to sanctifying grace through the sacramental presence of Jesus. They are not expelled from the Garden.

Next time you enter a Catholic church, breathe in deeply. You're back in the Garden!

Lesson 8

To make the most of this study, respond to all the questions yourself before reading these responses.

Firstfruits of the Fall (Gen. 4:1–7)

1. It should cheer us considerably to hear Eve's acknowledgment of God's gracious gift to her. She confirms for us that although man was weakened by sin, he was not in total darkness. It appears that, in Eve, the harsh punishment from God may have had a restorative effect. Was she humbled by being expelled from the Garden? Was she moved by the unmistakable sign of God's tenderness and care when He clothed her naked body with animal skins? Eve's statement about the birth of her son reflects the kind of humility that comes from true repentance. Adam and Eve proceeded with married life outside Eden; even if they were not the people they once were, God's mercy on them bore good fruit. Perhaps Eve's humble comment about the birth of "a man" with the help of the Lord reflected her understanding of the promise God made in Genesis 3:15. Was she already looking for the birth of a special baby boy?

2. When Cain got angry with God rather than falling down in repentance and sorrow because the Lord did not accept his inadequate worship, he revealed himself to be a man whose perspective was seriously flawed. He stood in the center of his world, overshadowing God Himself. Cain was firmly in the grip of intense spiritual blindness.

3. a. God told Cain that if he did not "do well," sin would be "couching at the door" and its "desire" would be to master him. The image here is of an enemy lying in wait, ready to attack a victim. If Cain refused to worship God appropriately, he would make himself more vulnerable to giving into sin again. Why? Because God designed our natures to be habitual; we are, literally, "creatures of habit." If we choose the good, that choice strengthens us to choose the good again. Choosing good becomes a habit. If, like Cain, we choose evil, that choice weakens us to choose evil again. Choosing evil becomes a habit.

b. *Challenge question:* Saint Paul warned the Roman Christians about the subtlety of sin and its power to enslave those who give themselves to it. What makes sin dangerous is that it not only breaks communion with God, but it becomes the master of the one who commits it. The Church refers to this as the "double consequence" of sin—one is eternal (a break in communion with God) and one is temporal (a weakened will, making it easier to sin again). That is why God gave such a sober warning to Cain.

4. The difference between Cain and Abel is the mystery of human freedom. Surely both men knew the story of creation and of the expulsion from a beautiful garden. They both inherited Adam and Eve's sinful nature. They were well aware of God and themselves. Yet one chose to serve God and one chose to serve himself. They were free to make their own decisions, just as their parents had been.

Cain Is Cursed (Gen. 4:8–16)

5. Instead of choosing to accept God's offer to put things right, Cain chose to plot the murder of his brother. Rather than putting to death the jealousy and anger that raged within himself, he allowed hate to grow into murder. He calmly laid a trap for Abel, inviting him to join him in the field, in the way a brother would. A brotherly gesture was the beginning of his betrayal (just as the kiss of a close friend would one day betray Jesus). This episode reveals to us how hard Cain's heart had grown. Even though God had made a profound offer of grace to him, he became even more resolved to do evil rather than good. This characteristic of sinful human nature constantly appears throughout the rest of Scripture. When God's grace—the fire of His love—comes near to some men, their hearts melt and become malleable. For others, however, the nearness of God's grace causes a hardening like clay in a kiln. Such was the case with Cain.

6. God gave Cain an opportunity to confess his sin and be accountable for it, just as He had done with Cain's parents in Eden. A Father's love always wants to hear an explanation of why things went wrong.

7. Cain lied to God, and then he became sarcastic. He disavowed any responsibility for his brother's welfare, throwing off any constraints on his autonomy. In his pride, Cain chose separation from God and from men.

8. a. Cain didn't show any remorse or even regret.

b. His primary concern was that he would suffer under his punishment and that someone would kill him.

9. Responses may vary. Perhaps it was Abel's blood crying out for mercy for Cain that spared his life. Perhaps it was God's desire that Cain have an opportunity to repent and return to His presence. It may have been God's purpose to reaffirm the sacred nature of human life, even when it strays far from God's design. No matter what caused it, God's preservation of Cain's life was an expression of His goodness and mercy, especially for sinners.

10. Responses may vary. In the previous question, we recognized God's desire for Cain's life to be spared, even though he was a murderer. We have also seen many other signs of His love for humans:

- God expected the best from Cain, since giving the best to God is what men were designed and created for; anything less than the best in man's relationship with God will mean that man is less than fully human. God's rejection of Cain's offering, calling him to something better, was a sign of His love for him.
- God extended to Cain a gracious offer to do the right thing and blot out the wrong that had gone before.
- God gave Cain clear warning about the subtle danger of giving in to sin, as a friend would warn another friend about an enemy lying in wait.
- God gave Cain an opportunity to confess his sin and ask for forgiveness.
- To punish Cain, God gave him what he wanted; thus Cain would have an opportunity to experience the consequences of the choices he made; this could perhaps have led to repentance and restoration.
- In preserving Cain's life, God indicated that He had not entirely given up on this rebellious son.

Two Cultures Develop (Gen. 4:17–26)

11. **a.** Lamech, who is the Bible's first polygamist, appears to have been a violent, arrogant man. He boasted to his wives that he had killed a man for wounding or striking him. He appointed himself to avenge a simple wound in a wildly disproportionate way. He reasoned that if God promised to avenge Cain's death "sevenfold" (4:15), he was justified in avenging himself, even for a very small offense, "seventy times seven."

b. Something must have gone very wrong among these people. They knew the details of their family history (how else would Lamech know to compare his deed with that of Cain?), but they had no knowledge of what the details *meant*. Because Cain, by choosing to be a murderer and liar, had been exiled from his family and the presence of the Lord, his spiritual blindness was not only perpetuated among his descendants, but it intensified. The father always teaches the son, either for good or for evil. This is how it is in families. Through the rest of Scripture we see, over and over, what traits develop among men who, for whatever reason, have shut their hearts away from the presence of the Lord. This is our first example of it.

12. Seth appears to have been a man who, upon learning his family heritage, decided "to call upon the name of the LORD." This indicated in him a reverence for God, a humility, and perhaps a human spirit like Abel's.

Lesson 9

To make the most of this study, respond to all the questions yourself before reading these responses.

Wickedness Reigns on Earth (Gen. 6:1–10)

1. a. Just as God could look at all His works in the beginning, at creation, and see that they were "very good," He could look at what man had made of his life on earth and see that it was "corrupt." Man's rebellion against God eventually resulted in violence against other men and perhaps against the living creatures who were created to help man. Man's abuse of his freedom grieved God to the heart, for it was far removed from man's original destiny. Because evil overcame the good among men, it had to be stopped. God would pass judgment on His wayward sons.

b. *Challenge question:* As God continued to reveal Himself within man's history, He showed that although He is patient with sinners, ready to forgive, and tender in His care of them, a time does arrive when, because He is just, He does execute judgment. Rebellion, wickedness, and evil cannot continue unchecked. This is a truth that will appear again and again throughout Scripture. The history of Israel is full of episodes of judgment upon sin, after a period of forbearance. Jesus spoke often of "the day of the Lord," when God, acting as the just Judge, calls everyone to account. The Flood is Scripture's first warning that man should never mistake God's patience and mercy as grounds for presumption. If the Lord is slow to punish sin, it isn't because He winks at it. As Saint Peter says:

> First of all you must understand this, that scoffers will come in the last days with scoffing, following their own passions and saying, "Where is the promise of His coming? For ever since the fathers fell asleep, all things have continued as they were from the beginning of creation." They deliberately ignore this fact, that by the word of God heavens existed long ago, and an earth formed out of water and by means of water, through which the world that then existed was deluged with water and perished. But by the same word the heavens and earth that now exist have been stored up for fire, being kept until the day of judgment and destruction of ungodly men. (2 Pet. 3:3–7)

2. *Challenge question:* For animals to have been included in the cleansing of the earth suggests the inseparable relationship between man and the rest of creation. The dominion God had given him had real meaning—when man went down, so did all the rest of the earth. This helps us to see clearly how all the elements of creation led up to the creation of man. He was not just one player among many. Without man, the rest has no meaning.

3. Responses will vary. It is never easy for a man to live righteously when everyone around him is wicked. It requires self-discipline, courage, and faith. In Hebrews, Noah is described as one who was warned about events "yet unseen." He built a huge ark in the middle of dry ground. What kind of confidence did he have in the unseen realities? It was profound. He did not live his life according to what he could see. He exhibited a detachment from the world around him, relying only on God's commands. Quite possibly he had to face ridicule or abuse from people who lived only according to the imaginations of their own hearts. This was heroic virtue. Truly, he was God's friend.

The World Saved through Noah (Gen. 6:11–22)

4. **a.** Responses will vary. One of the truths about God hardest to grasp is that the One who set the stars in the skies, who put limits on the seas, and who keeps the entire universe working also knows how many hairs are on our heads. The fact that we are not lost in the cosmos is a staggering reality. Noah's quiet faithfulness in the midst of great evil was not overlooked. God is aware of each human life. No moment is lost.

b. For God to preserve the race of human beings through one righteous man, even though nearly all had become entirely corrupt, was a powerful testimony to how precious in His sight human righteousness is. Goodness, in one man, was the victor over the evil of thousands. In this, Noah was a "type" of Jesus, whose righteous life conquered evil definitively for all eternity.

The Waters Subside (Gen. 8:1–12)

5. **a.** Responses will vary. It would have been natural for Noah and his family to be eager to get off that boat. Perhaps they did wonder why they had to wait so long, while nature ran its course. Maybe they thought about asking for a miracle or two to speed things along.

b. *Challenge question:* This is a question we should be willing to ponder from time to time. We could have asked it right after Adam and Eve left Eden. Why didn't God immediately send "the woman" and her "seed" to set things right? Surely Israel's long wait for the appearance of the Messiah was punctuated with cries of "How long, O Lord?" In our own day, the Church echoes what Saint John wrote two thousand years ago at the end of the Book of Revelation: "Come, Lord Jesus!" (22:20). A few miracles could certainly speed things along.

As difficult as it may be to accept, God carries out His plan for creation through natural and supernatural means. It must please Him to allow nature and human history to take time to arrive at their destination. When we bump up against this, it reminds us how much of God's work is mysterious and inscrutable to us. We must agree with the Psalmist: "Such knowledge is too wonderful for me; it is high, I cannot attain it." (Ps. 139:6) Sometimes it looks to us as if a miracle or two would be so much more efficient. God isn't aiming at efficiency. His desire for us is holiness. God, the Artist, works in the media of time, nature, and human history to create the perfection that is our destiny. It takes faith to believe that. Noah is our example.

6. a. When the dove did not return, Noah knew that all the waters had receded and that the earth could sustain human life again.

b. *Challenge question:* The Church helps us to see the Holy Spirit as the dove that looks for habitable ground. In the days of Noah, it was dry earth that the dove sought and finally found. The appearance of the dove with the olive branch was a sign that a new life for man on the earth was about to begin. At the baptism of Jesus, the Holy Spirit's descent on Him in the form of a dove was a powerful sign that the soil of the human soul was finally fit for the presence of God's Spirit once again (cf. Gen. 2:7). Is there any thought more beautiful than this?

"Go Forth from the Ark" (Gen. 8:13–22)

7. This language reminds us of God's charge to Adam and Eve to be fruitful and multiply. It prepares us for a renewal of the covenant God made in Eden and probably a code of behavior.

8. a. Noah offered a burnt offering to the Lord as soon as he got off the ark.

b. It pleased the Lord greatly to see a man live this way—not just the faith in his heart, but his public act of making an offering. God made a promise never to curse the ground again because of man.

c. *Challenge question:* Noah's life provided "rest" for all those who came after him. Never again would they have to fear a return to chaos on the earth. This is the first episode of God's people being saved through the faithful obedience of a human being. It will not be the last.

Lesson 10

To make the most of this study, respond to all the questions yourself before reading these responses.

A Blessing from God (Gen. 9:1–7)

1. a. The repetition of God's blessing, the command to be fruitful and fill the earth, and His provision of food in the second scene helps us to understand that God began a work of restoration after the purging action of the Flood. He wanted to return His creation to His original intention for it.

b. *Challenge question:* The significance of the differences between the two scenes is that, although God had taken the initiative to cleanse the earth of evil and make a fresh start, sin and its devastating effects have not been completely rooted out of creation. The harmony of the first creation had been broken; now the living creatures will fear man as he exercises dominion over them. The fear of creatures for man will be a reminder to him that he is not who he thinks he is and not at all whom he was meant to be. As painful as it is to experience this dread in animals, it is a great mercy to us. In our spiritual blindness, we can look very good in our own eyes. With the loss of grace in Eden, we simply cannot see the truth about ourselves. We have an amazing capacity to minimize our sin, forgetting our true destiny. A little bird hopping away from us in fear gives us a moment to see ourselves reflected in its eyes—we are not the holy creatures we were meant to be. In fact, we are scary. We need help.

2. Responses will vary. The prohibition against taking life, which was to be penalized by death, reflected the reality that violence and corruption had spread so thoroughly in the human community at the dawn of history that God had to send the Flood to purge it. God could not trust men to curb their appetite for violence. Now, in the renewed earth, He would use laws with drastic penalties to rein it in. We are to interpret this as a sober sign that whereas God left Cain to his own conscience, without requiring his life for his act of murder, now He must act with laws to preserve safety on earth.

3. Responses will vary. This taboo on blood reflected the value of all life, both human and animal. Even though God permitted man to eat animals, he was not thereby to be callous towards animal life. He was to continue to show respect for life, since it comes directly from the hand of God. Man in his spiritual blindness is subject to pride, in which he sees himself as the center of the universe. It is a short step from there to abusing elements in that universe to serve his own purposes. Prohibitions such as this kept that impulse in check.

The Sign of the Covenant (Gen. 9:8–17)
4. **a.** Responses will vary. Man, weakened by sin, had the potential to miss the messages God gave him. Was it possible that men would see the importance God attached to that beautiful rainbow and begin to worship it instead of God, who created it? Certainly. We know for a fact that men regularly worshiped what God created instead of the Creator Himself.

   b. *Challenge question:* God took that risk in order to communicate with man in a truly human way. As the *Catechism* says, "In human life, signs and symbols occupy an important place. As a being at once body and spirit, man expresses and perceives spiritual realities through physical signs and symbols. As a social being, man needs signs and symbols to communicate with others, through language, gestures, and actions. The same holds true for his relationship with God" (no. 1146). Scripture is full of examples of God working this way among His people. The culmination, of course, was the Incarnation, when God took on the most profoundly human form of communication—flesh and blood—to reveal to men who He is. That was risky, too. After all, if God became a Man, men could lay hands on Him and kill Him. God knows well the danger involved in His condescension to our humanity. He is not deterred.

The Sons of Noah (Gen. 9:18–29)
5. Responses will vary. We have seen a gardener abuse fruit before (in Eden). That did not produce a happy outcome.

6. Although we can't be sure of his exact offense, Ham appeared to have been severely lacking in respect for his father. If he was guilty of incest, it would demonstrate not just a lack of respect, but possibly an attempt to reject his father's authority. He may have boasted about his deed to his brother, always a sign of pride and arrogance; the boasting could have represented his attempt to usurp the rightful superiority of Shem, Noah's firstborn son.

7. Shem, the firstborn son, and Japheth, the youngest, went into the tent to make things right. They took every precaution to keep their father's dignity intact. Perhaps we can presume that because Shem was the oldest, he was the one who turned a bad situation away from complete disaster by having his youngest brother assist him rather than stay back and listen to more talk from Ham.

The Tower of Babel (Gen. 11:1–9)

8. a. These descendants of Ham reached a high degree of technical proficiency. This seems to have created a great deal of power among them. They did not want anything to threaten that power. They especially seemed to dread having to move out over the uninhabited parts of the earth. Perhaps they feared their power would dissipate if they got separated. Perhaps they didn't want to leave the comforts that came with civilization. Their desire to build a tower to heaven speaks of an arrogance and autonomy that has been dangerous when we have seen it in others (Adam, Cain, Lamech, Ham). The tower was a physical manifestation of the pride of man, a self-exaltation of men from earth to heaven.

b. God saw that because men had chosen to band together, refusing to spread out, the evil among them could grow without limit. The ease with which they could communicate made this possible. Their power to influence and intimidate each other meant that goodness could easily be overwhelmed by what comes most naturally to man, which is pride.

God responded by confusing the one language all men spoke at the time of the building of the tower. Whether they wanted to or not, the Lord scattered men over the face of the earth, separating them by languages and making unity difficult.

c. *Challenge question:* The diversity in human languages represents the pride and arrogance of man, who abused his original unity with others to work against God instead of for Him. On the day of Pentecost, when the Holy Spirit was poured out on the apostles to begin the work of creating the Church, it is of no small significance that there was a miracle that undid the effects of Babel (cf. Acts 2:1–13). It was a thrilling sign that God was creating a new unity on earth—a unity that would overcome the effects of sin and enable God's family to live as one, for His glory.

The Descendants of Shem (Gen. 11:10–32)

9. Terah and his family worshiped "other gods," according to the passage in Joshua. What does that mean? It is simply evidence that even in families that issued from a righteous man (in this case, Shem), there was always the possibility of confusion and contamination in their understanding and practice of the covenant. As we saw early in the history of man, intermarriage between cultures of different religious beliefs always presented problems to those whose heritage it was to live within the covenant. As the *Catechism* says, "The covenant with Noah after the flood gives expression to the principle of the divine economy toward the 'nations,' . . . toward men grouped 'in their lands, each with [its] own language, by their families, in their nations. . . . But, because of sin, both polytheism and the idolatry of a nation and of its rulers constantly threaten this provisional economy with the perversion of paganism" (nos. 56–57).

10. *Challenge question:* Responses will vary. If we think of the re-creation as an act of God to wipe out wickedness on the earth, it didn't work. But if we understand the Flood to be an act of divine revelation, it was everything it needed to be. First, it served as a demonstration that God does not restrain His judgment on sin forever. Men need to know this so they can live in truth. When men persist in their desire to be entirely free from God, eventually God gives them what they want. For them, God ceases to exist.

Second, it was a lesson for man in his own history that the solution to the wickedness of the human heart must be interior. Sin is inherent in his nature. It is systemic. The waters of the flood cleansed the earth of sinners, not of sin itself. It will take the waters of baptism to wash clean the human soul. "Baptism, which corresponds to this [the Flood] now saves you, not as a removal of dirt from the body but as an appeal to God for a clear conscience, through the resurrection of Jesus Christ" (1 Pet. 3:21).

Third, the re-creation is one in a very long line of episodes in Scripture in which the persistent longing of God for men is made crystal clear. In it, we saw His willingness to do whatever it takes to keep them in the covenant with Him. The promises He made to Noah and his sons gave them every reason to love Him back in the way He loved them. Frail mortals like us need to read these re-creation stories over and over until it finally sinks in—God will never give up until He has us for His own.

IT'S YOUR V.I.P. PASS TO THE GREATEST CELEBRATION OF ALL TIME . . .

THE MASS

Imagine 12 of today's top Catholic authors, apologists, and theologians collaborating on a book that answers *your* questions about the Mass. Now imagine that *you* have access to their collective knowledge, insight, and experience—right from your living room.

Imagine no more; it's a reality once again with *Catholic for a Reason III: Scripture and the Mystery of the Mass.*

Edited by Scott Hahn and Regis Flaherty, with a foreword by Bishop Robert C. Morlino, *Catholic for a Reason III* brings you such prominent Catholic authors as Scott and Kimberly Hahn, Jeff Cavins, Tim

Gray, Edward Sri, Curtis Mitch, Leon J. Suprenant, and others (yes, we're name-dropping). Each chapter explores the biblical foundation of the Mass in light of Church teaching, going to the heart of topics like "The Mass and Evangelization," "The Eucharist in the Apostolic Church," and "The Mass and the Apocalypse."

Catholic for a Reason III is bound to become an apologetics classic. Call (800) 398-5470 to order your copy today, or visit your local Catholic bookstore.

EMMAUS ROAD
PUBLISHING

(800) 398-5470 • www.emmausroad.org

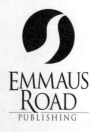